Architect?

The MIT Press
Cambridge, Massachusetts
London, England

Architect?

A Candid Guide to the Profession

Roger K. Lewis

Third printing, 1986

© 1985 by The Massachusetts Institute of Technology

This book was set in Helvetica and Palatino by Achorn Graphic Services and printed and bound by Halliday Lithograph in the United States of America.

Library of Congress Cataloging in Publication Data

Lewis, Roger K.
  Architect?: a candid guide to the profession.

  1. Architecture—Vocational guidance—United States.
I. Title.
NA1995.L45   1985   720'.23'73   84-23421
ISBN 0-262-12110-7
ISBN 0-262-62048-0 (pbk.)

For architects and architectural students who struggle to do their best, win or lose; and for those who have been most tolerant of my struggles and insensitivities— my family

Contents

I. To Be or Not to Be . . . an Architect?

II. Becoming an Architect

III. Being an Architect

This book about becoming and being an architect seems to be missing in the literature of architecture, a literature otherwise rich and plentiful. There are thousands of books on architectural monuments, movements, history, theory, design, drawing, technology, and management. Every year new publications spew forth covering cities, suburbs, construction, materials, graphics, homes, housing, hospitals, and hotels. The American Institute of Architects publishes handbooks for architects which describe concerns and methodologies of the profession, idealized prescriptions for practice intended for already educated architects. They contain useful checklists and standardized documents but reveal none of the agonies and ecstacies of being an architect. Indeed, I know of no single book that honestly informs prospective architects and architectural students of what to expect.

Believing the need for such a book to be real and widespread, I have tried to write a candid account of the realities of architectural education and practice. It is a subjective work based substantially on my own experiences, observations, and conclusions. I have tried to disclose the texture and complexity, the pros and cons, of being an architectural student and practicing architect. The book purposefully focuses on traditional architectural practice, since this is what most architects are educated for and what most prospective architects expect to do. Consequently I have avoided exploring the many diverse, sometimes marginally related fields that graduate architects enter in lieu of traditional practice.

For whom is this book written? Since finishing architectural school in 1967, I have taught and practiced architecture and advised, instructed, or employed hundreds of neophyte architects. Yet, I have not encountered anyone who had reliable, accurate notions of what he or she was really getting into, either prior to embarking on an architectural career or, in many cases, after embarkation. Years of answering the question, What's it really like to be an architect?, so often posed by students, clients, and others, have led me to attempt the story.

Therefore this book primarily addresses anyone seriously contemplating becoming an architect: students in high school and college, those out of school thinking about reentering, beginning architecture students, and young architects just finishing school. I hope that career guidance counselors and academic advisors will read or refer to this book before offering suggestions to their questing advisees. I hope architects' clients, or potential clients, will read it to learn the facts of life about the architects they hire, admire, or abuse. Finally, architects may want to read this book to see if it affirms or denies their own view of themselves and their personal experiences.

I have assumed at least two levels of readership interest. One level seeks basic information, whereas the other looks for basics plus elaboration and commentary. Thus I have tried to respond to this dual interest. However, readers may discover additional levels of intent and interpretation beyond these two. The occasional use of statistics, charts, lists, anecdotes, and illustrations should help illuminate or even validate some of the book's contentions, which nevertheless represent solely my point of view.

The table of contents reveals the specific topics treated within, but it says little of the tone or color which an author might be establishing. For me, writing this book allowed an exploration of contrasts. The inside story of architectural education and practice is one of dualities: success and failure, acceptance and rejection, satisfaction and disillusionment, stimulation and boredom. Characterizing the experience of architecture as bittersweet, cliché that it is, is fitting. Although my judgments may not be shared by all, most issues raised are at least genuine and consequential. And anyone who has read this book will have been told the unvarnished truth, like it or not.

Acknowledgments

Like most authors I am indebted to many people in many different ways. They contributed indirectly through association over the years, associations that continued my education and enriched my experiences as an architect. Too numerous to cite by name, they have been colleagues, clients, students, friends, and acquaintances. Much of the opinion expressed here started with my listening to and interpreting their thoughts, as well as my own, although I take full responsibility for all that's said and advocated.

More directly, I have enjoyed the support of the University of Maryland School of Architecture and its deans, John Hill and John Steffian. A sabbatical leave from teaching in spring 1982, my first in fourteen years, allowed me to conceptualize this book and begin writing in earnest. Some very good friends—Samuel Gorovitz, Frank Schlesinger, Judith and Stanley Hallet, John Hill, and others—provided invaluable observations, advice, and editorial suggestions. And during the past two years both my wife, Ellen, and my son, Kevin, have endured hundreds of hours of neglect and preoccupation on my part as I sat worshipfully in front of my computer/word processor; I am very grateful to them for putting up with it all.

In 1960, during a severe sophomore year slump, I decided suddenly to switch from physics to architecture at the Massachusetts Institute of Technology. I was nineteen. At age seventeen I had entered MIT to become a scientist or engineer, but by the fourth semester of college I faced the common dilemma of not knowing what to be or do. I only knew that I wanted to work in the tangible, three-dimensional world and that I would probably not find this in the subatomic, arcane world of physics.

I sought advice from family, friends, and teachers. Architecture was suggested because I had always enjoyed art and graphics, possessed drawing talent, and had demonstrated technical aptitude. I had never considered architecture before, since I knew nothing about it. Brief visits to MIT's architecture department further stimulated my interest, essentially because of the project drawings which I saw scattered about and pinned up on walls. In that stressful spring architecture seemed to be the answer.

Following my decision, the little information and insight I actually had about architecture proved no obstacle to exciting speculation. I could foresee a wonderfully romantic, exalted profession promising intellectual rewards, wealth and prestige, an amalgam of art and technology fused together by social idealism and creative energy. As an architect I would be marshaling diverse resources and mastering many disciplines to create artfully designed and executed buildings, each a monument to its architect's genius. I would be a generalist and a specialist at the same time, a recognized professional, a purveyor of culture as well as a renderer of services to a needy clientele.

Heroic names like Frank Lloyd Wright and Le Corbusier, accompanied by visions of skyscrapers and beautiful drawings, came to mind. A heady realm of aesthetics, construction, appreciative clients, respectful public, and newly awakened 1960s consciousness beckoned. It appeared that the architect was in the middle of it all, orchestrating a kind of real-world opera.

In retrospect, there is nothing unusual about the way I and most architects make our decisions to become architects. People choose careers for many reasons, often knowing relatively little about their chosen career at the outset. Many careers appear inscrutable or mysterious to the uninitiated, the nature of which is discovered only after initiation. Although architecture is no exception, its real attributes differ greatly from those so often ascribed to it. Countless students, clients, and consumers of architecture possess incredibly meager, if not erroneous, knowledge or comprehension of how architects think and function. Indeed, most people have notions about what accountants, bankers, pilots, doctors, truck drivers, attorneys, or plumbers do which better approximate reality than do their notions about architects.

Few people ever require an architect's services. Most don't even know an architect. What they might know is the explosive Howard Ruark, embodied on the silver screen by Gary Cooper in Ayn Rand's *The Fountainhead*; urbane, blue-eyed Paul Newman reading electrical diagrams in his office/boudoir in the *Towering Inferno*; the daddy in television's *Brady Bunch*; or the vengeful vigilante, portrayed by Charles Bronson in the movie *Death Wish*, whose primary project activity consisted of shooting hoodlums in the streets and subways of New York City (he eventually branched out to Chicago). But I can think of no popular account about an architect being an architect.

Thus what follows is an account which, though unlikely to become popularized, will tell would-be architects reasons for being or not being an architect, what being an architect means, and how to become one.

1

To Be or Not to Be . . .
an Architect?

1

Why Be an Architect?

Why be an architect? Deciding to become an architect should be a positive decision predicated on positive expectations. What then can one expect? What are the rewards and motivations that lead men and women to invest five to eight years in rigorous university and professional education, three or more years in apprenticeship, and subsequent decades pursuing architectural practice, teaching, scholarship, or research? This chapter tries to answer these questions.

Money and Life-Style

Let us begin with an obvious potential incentive to which most people can relate—money. We all discover at an early age that income is one of the things that any career or profession should provide. Of course there are many levels of earning, from survival to affluence, and each earning level offers corresponding life-style choices. Because architects are frequently associated with high life-style circumstances, people may assume that architects are affluent, well-to-do, big-income professionals. Some are. Most are not.

Although it is possible to achieve substantial wealth as an architect—and no doubt some architects pursue this as a primary personal goal—it is very improbable. Instead, most architects earn comfortable or modest livings, enjoying reasonable but limited economic stability and prosperity. Incomes in the profession of architecture are solidly middle class, comparable to school teachers, executive secretaries, mechanics, carpenters, salesmen, and nurses.

Architects begin their careers as wage earners drawing hourly, monthly, or annual salaries which reflect prevailing marketplace conditions. After several years of apprenticeship and further practice, they may become associates or principal owners of firms, either in partnership with others or as sole proprietors. Generally, larger firms provide larger incomes at all levels when contrasted with smaller firms. Thus partners in bigger, well-established offices tend to earn more than partners in firms whose practices are small. Likewise a newly employed draftsperson will probably be paid more by a large firm than by a small one.

Those architects who earn large incomes may live very well. Frequently they choose to live in interesting houses modishly decorated and furnished. They may travel to exotic places, go skiing or sailing, or escape to vacation cottages in the mountains or by the sea. They may collect art, entertain extensively, or support charitable causes and institutions. All of this costs money which most wage earners do not have.

For the majority of architects with less affluence, there are nevertheless ample life-style choices that are not so dependent on high incomes. Many architects find great satisfaction living modestly in cities, suburbs, small towns, or rural areas. Their life-styles may be more basic, even approaching subsistence at times, but they also enjoy flexibility and freedom of a kind not found chasing economic success, the cash flow treadmill which requires continuous movement and lubrication.

Some architects have discovered other means, outside of traditional architectural practice, to sustain themselves financially. In fact one could argue that the ideal way to practice architecture is not to be obliged to make a living at it. Thus architects have become real estate developers or construction contractors, sometimes making (or losing) much more money than they could from design practice. Architects teach in architectural schools where they can sometimes earn in nine months what they could earn in twelve in an office. Still others marry well, either by good fortune or design, thereby enhancing or stabilizing their family income through their spouses' assets or earnings. Of course the easiest route is to inherit money, but few are so endowed. Those who are can practice architecture as an impassioned hobby.

At times, earning money can be a serious problem for architects, and as we shall see later, adequate compensation is an ongoing problem for the entire profession. Unlike some businesses and professions, architecture is not a field to enter to become rich by today's standards. The odds are strongly against it. But you can earn a decent living at it most of the time, even if you are not exceptionally talented and if you don't mind a little belt tightening from time to time.

Social Status

Social status is another reason one might choose architecture as a career. An elusive notion at best, it implies the achievement of a certain elevated place in society's hierarchy of who people are and what they do. Social status is relative, meaningful only in comparison with other professions or vocations. Society assumes that architects are educated, that they are both artistically sensitive and technically knowledgeable. Society does not know exactly how architects operate, but it does know that they often create monumental designs for monumental clients. As a result architects may be well respected or admired by members of a social system who, unfortunately, think less of people they consider lacking in education, less talented, and less acceptable in the company of people of wealth, influence, or so-called breeding.

I make no argument here about the validity of pursuing social status. But we are all aware of status, and for many people high status may become a desirable and explicit goal. It is fulfilling and ego boosting to be respected, to be invited places and seen by people one admires, or to be praised by peers whose opinions one solicits. As professionals, architects generally associate with other professionals, with people in the creative arts or with people in business or government. In many cultures architecture is among the most respected of all professions. The United States is no exception. In its newsletter (Memo #658 December 26, 1983), the American Institute of Architects reported that "nearly half of today's Americans—especially college graduates younger than 45—have expressed an interest in architecture, according to recent research results . . . ." And any architect will tell you that countless numbers of times he or she has heard people say that they should have or could have become architects.

As a corollary to social status, the possibility of becoming part of the so-called establishment may motivate some architects. Read establishment to mean power structure within a community, town, or city, for rarely can architects become part of national power structures except for those created by academic and cultural elitists. Here, belonging to the establishment suggests having close connections to business and governmental interests, being seen as a force to be reckoned with among influential peers of the local realm.

Establishment status means having your name recognized by people you don't know, being asked to serve on boards and committees, being sought periodically by the press, and knowing what's going on behind the scenes—being an insider to the off-the-record deliberations which occur in all communities, large or small, and which invariably involve those who see themselves as the power elite. Clearly social and establishment status are closely linked.

Fame

Beyond achieving economic and social status there is the lure of fame. Fame may even come without wealth and, in architecture, often does. To become publicly recognized, if not celebrated, can be an end in itself above all others. Everyone can name at least one or two "famous" architects, and architects can name dozens of other famous architects. To be famous usually requires that an individual do something exceptional and that others see, judge, and, most important, report it to a receptive and interested audience, preferably on a national or worldwide scale. Exceptional deeds may be constructive or destructive, as long as they are exceptional and therefore noteworthy.

Most architects become famous in a gradual way by doing work which eventually gets recognized for its excellence. Often such work is seen as innovative or avant garde in its early stages, with subsequent stages being periods of refinement and variation. A few architects seek innovation with every project. In all cases fame is established and measured by professional consensus, as illustrated by the following item which appeared in the *Wall Street Journal* (May 26, 1982, p. 33):

MORE TOP TEN. Fifty-eight deans and heads of accredited schools of architecture recently listed this country's top architects of nonresidential structures. The overwhelming winner was I.M. Pei, who was mentioned by nearly half of the deans . . . Rounding out the top ten were Romaldo Giurgola, Cesar Pelli, Kevin Roche, Philip Johnson, Gunnar Birkerts, Michael Graves, Charles Moore, Edward Larrabee Barnes and Richard Meier.

All of these architects are well known to other architects, but few are well known to the public. Fifteen years ago the list would have been quite different, and fifteen years hence it will have changed again. And of course there are many more than ten top architects (imagine lists of the "top ten" lawyers, dentists, police chiefs, chemical engineers, dermatologists, or newspaper editors!).

For architects, fame and recognition come through the publicizing and publishing of what they do, say, or write. This means not only designing and building projects but also winning awards for projects and having them appear in journals, magazines, or newspapers. It means boosting and being boosted. Lecturing and writing about one's work and philosophy, being talked and written about by others, winning or judging competitions, all boost fame and thrust architects into the professional limelight.

Today events unfold so quickly that acts of provocation and revolution promise fame more readily. There appears now to be more explicit striving for notoriety and celebrityhood as ends in themselves. Architects, perhaps more than other professionals, consciously or subconsciously harbor a desire for fame, for so much of their work is public—what we do shows. Perhaps we are in a kind of show business. Being famous may have its problems, but it is a form of public certification, a validation of success and a salvation from anonymity. Who has not fantasized about making the cover of *Time* magazine? Not easily attainable, but possible. For architects, fame usually produces a desirable side effect: more clients and commissions. Pursuing fame just may be good business.

Immortality

Yet even fame may be insufficient, for it can indeed be fleeting. If we contemplate basic human drives, procreation and perpetuation come to mind. What better way to live forever than through the creation of potentially ageless and permanent structures, buildings which, even as future ruins, might tell future archaeologists, historians, and cultural legatees the story of who we were and what we did. Most people settle for their succeeding offspring and family heirlooms to memorialize themselves, but architects can leave behind architecture as memorials to themselves.

If this seems presumptuous, it is not intended to be. I believe that most creative individuals desire to make at least one thing which could last forever. I recall thinking about this explicitly when I was an architecture student making comparisons between architecture and other careers. Only architecture seemed to provide the opportunity to create something lasting and immortal. The architect, I thought, survives and endures with his or her work. Even if my name were forgotten, I would know that my constructed offspring was not.

I am sure that many architects share this immortality impulse, even if consciously denying or resisting it. Properly understood and channeled, it is a perfectly healthy impulse, not a conceit. A commendable work of architecture is, in part, a statement of and about its architect, the architect's progeny ultimately left behind. However, its parenthood must be attributed not only to the architect but also to the client and those who built it, and to the society and culture of which it was part.

Contributing to Culture

Good architects see themselves as more than professionals rendering services to fee-paying clients. Architecture is an expression and embodiment of culture, or cultural conditions. The history of architecture and the history of civilization are inseparable. By designing and building, architects know that they may be contributing directly to culture's inventory of ideas and artifacts, no matter how insignificantly. Thus the search for appropriate cultural achievement is an important motivation for architects.

Think about the past and bring to mind images of successive cultures and civilizations. One cannot help but see architecture in the mind's eye. Pyramids in Egypt, Greek and Roman temples, Gothic cathedrals, medieval castles and townscapes, Renaissance churches and squares, English houses and gardens, oriental pavilions, industrial-age cities and skyscrapers come into view. Architecture is an indispensable component of even the most unsophisticated cultures. If asked to describe the world of American Indians, what child would fail to sketch a teepee? Think of Neanderthals, and you will soon think of caves.

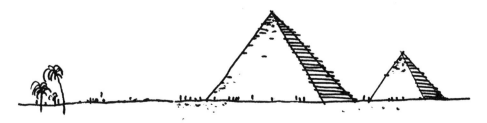

Unfortunately not all architectural work offers opportunities for cultural enrichment. But when such opportunities do arise, however modest, the architect's contribution may be unprecedented, suggesting new directions in style, technology, or methods of design. Or the work may reaffirm or refine already established cultural icons. Rather than inventing something new, the architect may simply be adding to the growing collection of cultural works completed or in progress. Innovation and revolution require subsequent development and evolution; architects must cover the field.

Helping and Teaching Others

Another of the architect's satisfactions may derive from humanitarian motives, among others. The desire to help or teach other people can be very strong, and since architecture can both render public service and serve as public art, architects can easily fulfill this desire. Many architects view themselves as benefactors to society, as humanists and humanitarians. Even when designing commercial projects for profit-motivated clients, architects believe that they have an additional, equally important client—the public. They feel an obligation to all who may use, occupy, or see the buildings they design, both in the present and the future—an obligation not only to provide shelter and accommodate activities but also to instruct and inspire.

When buildings are finished and put into use, it is very fulfilling for the architect to know that the client and the public appreciate and benefit from his or her efforts. Sometimes architects are able to create environments that truly affect the lives of people in positive ways, perhaps by improving their living standards, their behavior, their sense of well-being or security, or their attitudes. What a tremendous reward it is for architects to hear clients or users express satisfaction and gratitude for the architects' successful intervention in their lives.

Public-spirited architects contribute in ways other than designing buildings. Being adept in matters of organization, coordination, and advocacy, some architects have been successful in assisting needy individuals, communities, and special-interest groups to develop projects, preserve buildings, or save neighborhoods. Although the architect in these situations may not produce drawings, his or her efforts and know-how may lead to worthwhile building or enhanced environmental sensitivity. Like fame, yet in a very different manner, doing for others elevates our ego and validates our sense of achievement.

Teaching is giving, and it's an activity that can be very rewarding for architects, although not necessarily financially. It offers the dual satisfaction of professing and conveying knowledge to others, on the one hand, while receiving stimulation and appreciation, on the other. Academic freedom and flexibility of schedule allow teachers of architecture to practice, write, travel, or conduct research, as well as teach. Thus motivated teachers provide an exchange function, taking in or developing new ideas and information and then in turn passing them on to their students. Such interaction can be profound and enduring. One of teaching's greatest rewards in fact can come when teachers see their former students successfully applying what they have learned or following in their mentor's footsteps. Nothing compares with hearing a student tell you that what you conveyed at some earlier time is still remembered, still relevant, and still appreciated.

The Rewards of Creativity and Intellectual Fulfillment

Implicit in all of the architect's activities is the force of human intellect. But human emotions operate as well in all that we do. For architects the marriage of intellect and emotion is manifest in the impulse to be creative, to think, feel, do, and make. Perhaps one of the most convincing reasons to be an architect is the purely intellectual and emotional gratification which surrounds creativity.

The creative impulse is difficult to rationalize but easy to recognize. It appears early in life and is experienced by all human beings. To begin with nothing but raw materials and random thoughts, and later to transform them into something tangible, well crafted, and stimulating to the mind and senses, is the essence of creativity. For the architect, creating buildings can be a real "turn-on," a "high," a moment of elation.

Creating something beautiful or aesthetically composed—a work of art—is the primary goal of many architects. Their chief concern is to design buildings to look at and admire as one would look at and admire paintings or sculpture. Even if others dislike the design, the architect's eye still beholds the beauty which he or she alone has bestowed on the world through creative building.

Of course creativity is not limited to generating works of art. The creative mind takes pleasure in making things that work, whether buildings, machines, or toys. A substantial part of practicing architecture consists of creating physical environments that perform successfully. In other words, in addition to being artistic expressions, buildings must creatively accommodate human functions, be buildable from many components and materials, provide shelter from the elements, resist the forces of nature, and be affordable. Therefore meeting both performance and aesthetic objectives simultaneously is architecture's greatest creative challenge.

Once that challenge is taken up, the excitement of design is matched only by the excitement of realization. Seeing one's design actually constructed is both an emotional and intellectual experience because we feel excited as we interpret and rationalize design ideas being crafted in three dimensions. The rewards found in responding to creative impulses are further intensified by the struggles that accompany creativity. As we shall see later, overcoming adversity absorbs much of an architect's energy, for there are many obstacles in the path along which architects and their projects travel. Sometimes just getting a project built is a victory, but when it's good architecture, the victory is relished even more.

Architecture must accomplish many things for many different people, and diverse skills are required of architects to deal with the complexities of the design and construction process. Thus some of the intellectual fulfillment of practicing architecture lies in applying diverse skills to complex processes and problems. Intelligent, rational minds often take great pleasure in solving puzzles, organizing systems, and accomplishing specific tasks that have intellectual and artistic merit. Architecture provides fertile ground for such minds to plow.

Let's examine the array of intellectual opportunities hinted at here. Architecture entails activities of both mind and body acting in concert—thinking, drawing, crafting, seeing. The architect must know not only how to draw a line but also why and when. The senses must all be engaged to observe so that the mind can analyze and synthesize. Ideas must be communicated and explained graphically and verbally. What then are the specific aptitudes or talents that contribute to mastering and enjoying the discipline of architecture?

Graphic and visual skill The ability to "see" and to express things in graphic form.

Technical aptitude Proficiency in mathematics and scientific analysis (not necessarily in a particular science).

Verbal skills The ability to read, write and speak, to organize or analyze effective verbal expression.

Organizational skill The ability to create order and direction out of disorder and chaos.

Memory The ability to store and recall information or ideas.

Compositional talent The artistic ability to compose aesthetically successful visual form in two and three dimensions.

These are all essential to being an architect, prerequisites for intellectual fulfillment in architecture. They also reflect the multidisciplined nature of the field, the need for architects to be artists, craftspersons, draftspersons, technologists, social scientists, managers, accountants, historians, theoreticians, philosophers, gamblers, and other things to boot. Mobilizing talents in an arena so rich and diverse can be tremendously exhilarating and rewarding, as stimulating as any career could be.

Love of Drawing

Although our discussion of creativity and intellectual fulfillment talks briefly of the rewards of graphic exploration and invention, a further note about drawing itself seems appropriate. For many architects drawing is an extremely satisfying and stimulating use of time and energy, an activity that is, again, its own reward.

Drawing can be loved. It can be therapeutic, requiring great concentration and the masking out of all other distractions or preoccupations. It is personal, since no two people draw exactly alike. The most vital kind of drawing, and probably the most enjoyable, is sketching, as opposed to drafting. Sketching is the most spontaneous, the most plastic, and the most interpretive kind of drawing. Through sketching, architects both record impressions and express new ideas or visions. Drafting transforms sketched ideas into analogs of reality.

Drawing architectural forms—buildings, spaces in buildings, landscapes, urban spaces, or furniture—has to become as natural for an architect as writing or reading. In fact many architects would probably prefer to sit and draw, if given the choice, than to do most of the other things which architectural practice demands. Often the romance with drawing is taken to extremes. Architects may produce drawings whose qualities outweigh those of the design represented by the drawings. Some designers and draftsmen will spend more time crafting and rendering the drawings themselves than they spend developing and perfecting their architectural ideas. And we frequently see architects' drawings that are so seductive, so artfully composed, so evocative that we overlook the merits of the subject depicted by such drawings.

If you like drawing per se, and particularly freehand drawing, then you may grow to love it as an architect. If you don't like to draw, if you find it tedious or difficult, then architecture may

not be the right choice. In many ways the passion for drawing, and the drawing techniques which architects develop and master, are unique to the profession of architecture.

Fulfilling the Dictates of Personality

In looking at reasons to be an architect, we cannot overlook attributes of personality and their role in shaping architects' careers. These attributes may be disregarded or underestimated by students and counselors, but they are of great importance in determining career choices and directions. For in the real, day-to-day world outside the classroom, personal characteristics—let us say personality—may have greater influence on one's life than all of the intellectual skills, talents, and knowledge that one possesses. The rewards in architecture, like most professions, depend as much on personal and behavioral traits as on IQ, college transcripts, or good intentions.

Which personal attributes matter, since they are so many and so varied in everyone's personality? Of course they all matter, but some matter more than others. A sampling follows:

Self-confidence and ego strength Believing that you are capable, able to compete, perform well, and succeed.

Ambition Wanting vigorously to accomplish and succeed.

Dedication and persistence Committing and sticking to a cause or task, with a willingness to work hard at it.

Resilence Coping well with setbacks, criticism, failure; being able to bounce back, to overcome.

Amiability Being able to affiliate and get along with others (who are not close friends), to collaborate and participate.

Empathy Recognizing, understanding, and identifying with the circumstances and feelings of others.

Charm and poise Behaving so others see you as well-mannered, witty, thoughtful, friendly, comfortable to be with.

Leadership Being able to persuade and inspire others to follow you or embrace your proposals, and to make decisions, however well informed or ignorant.

Courage Willingness to take risks others shun, to experiment, to venture into new territory, to lose as well as win.

Passion Capacity for intense and emotional feelings about people, ideas, places, or things . . . easily taken for obsession.

This inventory does not constitute a complete list of requirements for being an architect, nor is it unique to architecture. However, measured doses of all of these attributes seem to be present in many good architects. And the lack of some of these attributes can prove to be a serious liability to achieving architectural goals, or even to becoming an architectural school graduate. In a discipline where criticism and negative judgments abound, lacking confidence and resilience and persistence can be devastating, notwithstanding one's native talents.

By contrast, an architect of mediocre talent, but blessed with great charisma (an amalgam of several attributes, especially leadership, self-confidence, and "magical" charm), may always do very well. Such charisma may have more impact on an architect's career than any measurable competencies learned in an educational program. The ability to sell and to guide other people may ultimately accomplish more for you than the ability to draw, calculate, or even think great thoughts.

Anyone contemplating architecture as a profession should seriously take stock of his or her personality. With assorted combinations of individual traits, and in appropriate intensities, architecture can be the ideal profession in which to capitalize on such traits. Indeed, one occasionally meets people who seem to have been born to be architects, who seem to possess a mixture of intellect, talent, skills, and personal qualities—some of which are unquestionably genetic in origin—that makes architecture their undeniable "cup of tea."

Freedom to Do Your Own Thing

Perhaps because architects are thought of as "creative" and "artistic," society accepts their periodic departures from conventional behavior and attitudes, or even expects it at times. Many architects do live up to their image, exhibiting idiosyncracies in the ways they dress, talk, and work, or in their beliefs. They strive to be individualistic and nonconformist, if not radical. Frank Lloyd Wright, wearing his reputed cape and haughty expression, defied and decried all, becoming a prototype for iconoclastic architects.

Thus for anyone so inclined, architecture may be more attractive as a career than, say, banking, accounting, or military service. There is a kind of ego satisfaction and reassuring feeling of exceptionality which comes from being unique and different, from standing out, getting noticed and being remembered.

Architects appear to have more options for doing their thing their way in our culture, especially in comparison to other learned professions. They seem to have more freedom to shape and control the image of themselves which they project to their peers, their clientele, and the public. This is reinforced by the work they do, the architectural values they espouse, the people with whom they associate, the causes they support, and the style in which they live. Few careers offer this range of choice in how one behaves and practices. Almost anything goes in architecture if it is done with panache. For this reason architecture may be the most liberal of the established professions, the most tolerant and encouraging of deviation.

Finally, there is yet another reason for being an architect. Many architects really know how to have a good time, to let go when necessary. Starting first as students indulging in absurdities in school, architects have always found imaginative ways to relieve the pressure and stridency of architectural work. The fun comes through being whimsical, creating visual anecdotes or puns, and designing fantasies, as well as through more conventional recreational means. But the good times and amusing diversions are needed for still another purpose. As the next chapter explains, architecture has its negative side, and having a good time can help cope with bad times.

2

Why Not to Be an Architect

It may seem heretical and treasonous to the profession of architecture to cite reasons not to be an architect, much less devote a whole chapter to it. But the story would be both incomplete and misleading if it failed to include the less-than-wonderful aspects of being an architect. Whenever we are told why we should do something, there may be unstated reasons why we should not. This is reinforced by experience, sometimes painfully. Painting the entire picture of becoming and being an architect at least gives the reader the chance to make informed decisions, to accept or reject, without feeling that there has been misrepresentation.

Reasons not to be an architect are a matter of judgment. Therefore what follows are my own observations and interpretations of commonly encountered risks, roadblocks, and sources of frustration. Some are typical of many trades or professions, while others are more unique and endemic to architecture. It is safe to suppose that at one time or another virtually every architect has been plagued by some or all of these problems, felt overwhelmed or disillusioned by them. Unfortunately knowing about and anticipating them makes them no less obstructive.

The Odds of Making It

Anyone contemplating a career in architecture should first know that there may be less than a fifty-fifty chance of ultimately becoming a licensed architect, should he or she begin architectural school in the coming year. A minority of the students who enroll annually in American architectural schools can expect to complete the professional program and receive an accredited degree in architecture. The Association of Collegiate Schools of Architecture (ACSA) reported in its January 1983 "ACSA News" that the National Architectural Accrediting Board (NAAB) released a compilation of statistics for accredited architectural programs for the 1981–82 academic year which included the following:

Full-time equivalent students enrolled	**1981–82**	**30,544**
Graduates of accredited programs	1980–81	4,498
	1979–80	4,443
	1978–79	4,153

This clearly implies and illustrates that many architectural students drop out, since the ratio of those graduating to those enrolled is about one to seven, whereas one might expect it to be one to four, on the average, without attrition.

Moreover not all of those graduating from accredited schools with accredited professional degrees will become registered and practice architecture. Some will change fields for various reasons, usually related to their feelings about their prospects as architects. They may be attracted to other fields for economic reasons, or because they have other talents more suitable to other career options. Regrettably, some women with architectural degrees stop working indefinitely in order to have families, finding it difficult to pursue their careers in architecture at the same time.

Ironically, although student attrition and dropping out is high, there is no shortage of architects in the United States, especially in urban areas where most projects are built. Many architects, and some educators, believe that there are in fact too many architects and too many architectural firms. In addition surveys of firms conducted by the American Institute of Architects (AIA) show that approximately one-fourth to one-third of architects in firms are owners or principals (proprietors, partners, or corporate officers). In other words, the majority of working architects are employees, not employers.

How do we interpret these statistics? They suggest a low probability that someone setting out to be a practicing architect will end up being an architect, and an even lower probability that they will actually become owners or principals of firms. Such statistical chances are not very encouraging. Yet we know that attrition and unrealized goals are normal in any academic undertaking or career, that people change their minds and majors with ease and regularity. But attrition in architecture is unusually pronounced, and those who make it through and enter practice, despite the odds, still face tough challenges.

Lack of Work

Of all the difficulties faced by architects, periodic lack of work is probably the most frustrating. The inability of individuals to find employment, or of firms to obtain commissions, is a major cause of economic and psychological suffering for practicing architects.

Employment for firms and individuals is directly related to both local and national economic conditions. When times are good and economic growth occurs, income, savings, and investment increase. Investing in building likewise increases, which means architects get busier. Correspondingly lack of economic growth, recession, inflation, and high interest rates diminish incomes, savings, and investment. Building activity diminishes as well, and with it, architectural commissions diminish. Therefore the overall amount of work for architects is determined by the volatile and unpredictable conditions of the economy over which architects have no control. The architect must constantly face the possibility of being under- or unemployed from one year to another.

Lack of work can also result from more localized conditions which the architect is unable to influence. Even if the general economy is strong, municipal or state economic circumstances may be unstable or in decline. Since architects' work is organized on a project-by-project basis, their employment fate is intimately linked to the fate of each client and project. Architects are hired by clients when projects are conceived and laid off when projects are suspended or terminated.

Projects are financed by lending institutions or government agencies, built by contractors, and bought, leased, or used by the public. Thus the building process is complex, and for many reasons projects can start and stop very quickly. Because so much time and money can be invested in the architect's work on any single project, even the loss of one or two can be economically disastrous to a firm. Were architects rendering services to hundreds or thousands of clients at a time, this risk would be greatly reduced. But with most offices only working on a few projects over many months or years, the risk of not having work is increased.

Sometimes work can fall off dramatically. Recall that in 1974 economic expansion that had been steadily continuing for almost three decades, with only minor abbreviated recessions, abruptly ended. Architects were laid off at a rate not seen since the depression era of the 1930s. In my own office I was forced to let go most of my professional staff, a dozen architects, when work suddenly stopped in late 1973 and 1974. It was an agonizing act of retrenchment. Some firms became mere shadows of their former selves, shrinking by 70 or 80 percent.

In Cambridge, Massachusetts, on a day referred to as ''black Friday,'' one of the country's largest and most prestigious architectural firms laid off close to one hundred employees because projects were suddenly stopped. Fortunately this is not a typical, everyday occurrence. Further architects tend to be mobile, moving from firm to firm with rising and falling work loads, as well as for personal reasons. Employment follows projects, an inescapable fact of architectural life.

Competition

The threat of having no work is made worse by another ever-present factor, intense competition. As if normal economic uncertainty were not enough, there is the problem of too many architects chasing too few jobs. Competition in the field of architecture is keen and unending. It begins in school, carries over into the beginning years of job seeking and employment, and continues in the marketplace of practice.

Competition is certainly not unique to architecture, being integral to any free enterprise system. But in architecture it can reach astounding proportions. For example, in the period following the 1973–74 oil embargo and recession, it was not uncommon to see as many as one hundred firms competing for a single, small, government project pursuant to an agency announcing that it was looking for architects. When times are tough, architects can spend months looking unsuccessfully for jobs, simply because the number of competitors is so great in comparison to the amount of available work. In such interims architects may be forced to survive on unemployment benefits.

The intensity of competition is due to not only an apparent oversupply of architects but also the methods by which architects compete with one another. Architects are challenged by their colleagues in two ways: first, by their sheer numbers and, second, by their ability and willingness in many cases to mount effective, aggressive campaigns to woo clients. Competing successfully today implies both soft and hard selling, the tactics of marketing and public relations. Such tactics may prove distasteful to some architects.

Inadequate Compensation

In chapter 1 I talked briefly about earning money in architecture, indicating that it is possible, but unlikely, for architects to earn above-average incomes. Indeed, no one should go into architecture to make a lot of money. Be an architect for many other reasons but not to get rich.

The reader has probably realized that given the numbers of architects and the competition, financial remuneration accompanying architectural employment may not be the greatest. Typically most architects believe that they are not adequately compensated and certainly not well compensated for what they do. The 1983 AIA Registered Architects Survey asked respondents if "you feel that in comparison to other professions, architects receive adequate fees for services they provide?", and 85.7 percent said no. When asked if "you feel that employers compensate their architect employees adequately?", 67 percent answered no.

Architects can earn enough most of the time to live comfortably, but few will ever match income and assets with their contemporaries who practice medicine, law, engineering, or accounting, or with executives in business and government. Architects may have more fun, but they will probably have less money. Table 2.1 shows the scope of architects' income in recent years, and table 2.2 lists incomes for other occupational categories. Inspecting these statistics clearly reveals that architecture is generally a low-paying profession in comparison to others.

Keep in mind that for many architectural firm owners, annual income can fluctuate widely. A good year can be followed by several bad years, years in which a principal's income could be at the poverty level, or could be negative (a loss). Architects' dependency on economic and project circumstances differentiates their income pattern from that of doctors or lawyers, whose earnings consistently increase over time and who stay busy whether times are good or bad. Moreover the vast majority of established architects do not earn incomes significantly greater than the median, which is not the case for established professionals in other fields.

Part of the compensation problem was put into lucid perspective by another survey done by the AIA, the 1981 firm survey. I quote from a section entitled "Architects Compensation in Perspective" and have included appropriate survey data:

Table 2.1
Architects' base compensation (AIA firms)

Staff	Median base salary[a] 1981	1970	Percent increase, 1970–1980 Architecture	Miscellaneous professions	Construction workers	Consumer Price Index
Principal	31,249	20,310	55			
Supervisory	24,000	13,200	82			
Technical 1	18,538	10,890	70	195[b]	114[b]	140
Technical 2	14,414	8,860	63			
Technical 3	10,714	5,790	85			

Source: "The 1981 AIA Firm Survey," The American Institute of Architects, April 1982.
Note: Principal: owner, partner, corporate officer. Supervisory: general manager, department head, project manager, project architect, project engineer. Technical 1: senior technical staff—frequently licensed, highly skilled specialist, job captain, senior designer, senior planner, senior specifier, senior construction administrator. Technical 2: intermediate technical staff—usually not licensed, including intermediate levels of positions listed under Technical 1, management or clerical staff. Technical 3: junior technical staff—not licensed, including junior levels of positions listed under Technical 1, clerical staff, office assistant.
a. The average of the median base salaries is $19,819!
b. Data for 1970–79 increase.

Nominal or current-valued total compensation has increased over the period 1970–81 by 59 percent for principals, 80 percent for supervisors, 66 percent for Technical I staff, 57 percent for Technical II staff and 70 percent for Technical III staff [based on the data in table 2.1] . . . inflation measured by the Consumer Price Index (CPI) has risen 140 percent since 1970 . . . it is apparent that real income for principals and all other staff in architecture firms has declined both nationally and regionally.

. . . comparing the increases in principals' compensation with increases in construction wages and salaries and compensation for miscellaneous professional services for the 1970–81 period . . . Again, compensation for architects has not kept pace with increases in compensation of other workers in the construction industry as well as some of their professional brethren, including engineers, land surveyors, accountants and auditors.

Since these two comparison measures show that there has been a markedly poor performance in the growth of income for architects over the past decade, it is important to search for expla-

Table 2.2

1981 Earnings, year-round full-time male and female workers

Occupation	Median earnings	
	Male	Female
Accountants	24,905	15,631
Computer specialists	26,765	19,340
Engineers	31,069	a
Scientists	29,810	a
Physicians, dentists	38,504	a
Self-employed physicians	46,533	a
College teachers	27,429	20,978
Managers and administrators		
Manufacturing	30,444	16,880
Retail	19,424	12,452
Finance, insurance, and real estate	29,424	15,452
Federal government	30,062	a
Sales workers (insurance, real estate, stocks)	24,968	13,696
Clerical workers	18,938	11,755
Blue-collar workers		
Construction crafts	19,178	a
Service workers	14,010	8,310

Source: U.S. Bureau of the Census, "Money Income of Households, Families, and Persons in the United States: 1981," Government Printing Office, Washington, D.C.

a. Sample size less than 75,000 workers. Note that females earn less than males in all categories; this is also true in architecture.

nations. One possible source for answers is an analysis of the financial health of the construction industry itself . . . In particular, the real value of public building construction has decreased by 32.8 percent (since 1970). Further, the real values of total private construction and private, nonresidential building construction have increased by only insignificant rates of 2.1 percent and 7.9 percent, respectively, . . . the performance of the construction industry in increasing the real economic value of all structures built has been distinctly unimpressive.

The economic performance of the construction industry over the past decade has been poor. Yet in spite of this poor performance, along with inflation, workers in the construction industry as a whole have been able to increase their compensation considerably. The question that requires further research is why architects have not been able to realize a similar accomplishment.

A good question. One must conclude that for whatever reasons, architects as a whole are unable to claim compensation appropriate to their role. The same points are always raised: so many years of education! demonstrable and unique expertise! a recognized, learned profession regulated by law! an activity encumbered by substantial legal and financial risks which in turn justify fair compensation and profits! Why then are so many architects apparently paid so poorly?

As noted earlier, supply and demand relationships are a major contributor to the problem, with too little work for too many architects. Architectural fees are frequently too low, or they go uncollected, flowing in unpredictable currents, just like projects. But why should fees be too low, given the architect's qualifications, risks, and efforts? The answer is competition. In the marketplace there is always pressure to quote fees that are at least comparable to the going rates, and often to cut fees below the going rates, which then lowers the going rate another notch. Clients go shopping for architects and rarely hesitate to ask about cost of services. If a hungry architectural firm is anxious to secure a project commission, the temptation to propose a cut-rate fee can be overwhelming, even when it means cutting corners, compromising on the quality of services, spending less time than needed, and paying slave wages to employees.

Many architectural practitioners feel trapped. On the one hand, as competent professionals they would like to invest all of the time and resources necessary to research thoroughly, discover, and describe the best possible design and to see that it is properly implemented. This implies that clients must share the architect's goals and visions and be willing to compensate them fully for the value of all required services. On the other hand, many architects' real-world experience teaches them that clients may view them as just another vendor among competing vendors, clients who believe architectural fees to be excessive, yet who want flawless, complete work at below cost.

In the future it is unlikely that architects can expect to improve significantly their earning power without changing the supply-demand relationships and without insisting on full and adequate compensation, despite what the competition is doing. In a free market system the consumer of architectural services—and the architectural employer—will undoubtedly find sufficient numbers of warm bodies and firms eager and willing to work for the most minimal fee. No matter what price is proposed, there is always an architect somewhere who will do the work for less, and promising as much or more.

To the established architect or firm, this situation is a mixed blessing. Although intense competition for projects makes it harder to survive, the ample supply of architects, both young and old, allows firms to keep their labor costs and fees as low as possible, since most architectural fee revenue is spent on staff salaries. In fact the current economic structure of architectural practice depends on this exploitation of labor to provide services that are, by their nature, extremely labor intensive. A project can consume thousands of worker-hours.

It is worth reminding ourselves, before concluding this discussion of compensation, that the points made are all relative. In other words, architects seem underpaid only when they are compared to certain others in our society. They can earn more than some people ever hope to earn and frequently earn more than teachers, scholars, musicians, actors, and artists doing work which may be equally creative and fulfilling. It is even possible to out-earn plumbers, truck drivers, attorneys, and doctors, if that is your goal as an architect—but it's not easy.

Ego Vulnerability: Getting Lost in the Crowd

The level of ego involvement in architecture is high, and this can lead to great frustration as well as provide the impetus for achieving. To most architects succeeding means, among other things, gaining some measure of professional standing and reputation, if not fame. There is a natural craving for peer group recognition, even beyond one's clientele and income, for having done well, for being in some way exceptional.

Yet in actuality many architects feel, rightly or wrongly, that they have failed to gain the status or recognition that they deserve. They toil away as employees, associates, or principals in firms, carrying on the demanding, day-to-day work of producing architecture, while a handful of their colleagues receive most of the attention and credit. Some perceive themselves as anonymous cogs in a giant system over which they have limited control. They feel unjustly treated and passed over.

Visit a large architectural office where there might be fifty or a hundred architects working. It would not be surprising if many of them characterized themselves as unfulfilled, underappreciated, underpaid, and overworked architects with lots of talent

and little luck. Some feel exploited, chained to their drafting boards and jobs, unable to make that breakthrough to stardom, to freedom. Most will have successfully completed professional educations, many will be licensed, and all will have differing but important forms of talent, indispensable to architectural practice. A few will feel cheated or deprived by external forces. Others will feel that they suffer from some combination of personal inadequacies that prevents them from doing or achieving more, resigning themselves to anonymity and content just to do their best. Still others will be dreaming and waiting for the right moment, the right opportunity, to emerge from the crowd.

The Risks of Envy

Why should architects feel or think this way? Why does this sound like a description of aspiring actors in New York or Hollywood, rather than a group of highly trained, licensed professionals? Is this condition particularly acute in architecture? As the first chapter makes clear, fame and status, a kind of stardom or eminence, seem to be aspirations in architecture. Or the lack thereof implies that one's work is incompetent, uninteresting, passé, or otherwise unworthy of notice. Hence there is an inescapable pressure on architects which motivates them but which can also produce feelings of jealousy or envy. Professional jealousy can arise in all lines of work, but it may be more keenly felt in architecture. Given the competition and egos that prevail, it is easy to understand why architects fall victim to these sins.

Envy and jealousy rarely surface in public. They are privately felt and coped with. They can appear whenever an architect observes some other architect winning while the observer is losing or is left out. They are beyond normal feelings of frustration or disappointment. Rather, they manifest themselves in a subtle but gnawing, slightly malicious way, sometimes accompanied by a bit of ill will and resentment of the comparative success of others. Paradoxically, architects may have parallel feelings of respect and admiration for their envied competitors and peers. Professional jealousy is an unfortunate, regrettable dimension of the architect's ego, rarely acted upon externally, but capable of precipitating internal damage to the psyche.

Anything can trigger such feelings, especially at moments of vulnerability: seeing others busy when you are not; others winning awards or competitions when you are not; others being published or favorably reviewed when you are not; others being promoted when you are not; others making money when you are not. The negative stimuli can be unending. Losing a job or a commission you thought you should have gotten, or falling out of fashion as fashions change, can provoke and embitter. These sentiments are not restricted to young, immature, or unsuccessful architects. Indeed, every architect is susceptible, and the higher one's aspirations, the higher the susceptibility.

Anxiety and Depression

Jealousy is a normal symptom, and so is professionally related depression, to which architects are easily prone from time to time. Many things can cause depression, mostly relating to failure or impending failure. Lack or loss of work, financial setbacks, or inadequate recognition can do the job. This suggests that in order to be a happy architect, one must be emotionally tough. Conversely, don't be an architect if you suffer from severe rejection anxiety or fear of failure, for periodic failures are guaranteed in the practice of architecture.

Anxiety and depression over money matters are commonplace, experienced and understood by all, and certainly not unique to architecture. But as professional designers, architects produce work that is continually scrutinized, tested, criticized, redone, and frequently rejected. Trite as it sounds, it comes with the territory. No one likes rejection, but architects must be especially able to accept and cope with it. This is not always easy. Imagine the feelings that can well up when, after pouring perhaps hundreds or thousands of hours into a design, you are told that your work is unacceptable, or worse, that it's terrible. Rejection and failure are bitter medicines to swallow, but every architect has tasted them, no matter how unjustifiably.

Rejection does not mean necessarily that extraordinary talent and effort have not been applied in creating an architectural design. Brilliant labors of love are rejected all the time, along with mediocre ones. However, judgment of architecture is based on the values and taste of those who are judging. Judgments get made for political, social, and economic reasons totally beyond the architect's powers of anticipation and control. So the architect has little choice but to endure these recurring circumstances, always exerting his or her best, or to drop out. Dropping out may appear to be the best alternative for avoiding depression only when compensating successes seem unattainable.

Personal Encumberances

Architecture demands taking risks. It demands great investment of time, effort, and emotional and physical energy to achieve anything worthwhile. To be able to seize opportunities when they arise, or to pursue unconventional goals, requires both personal resources and a certain degree of freedom from personal encumberances.

In particular, starting one's own architectural firm is often a great risk, especially financially. Yet it is the objective of most architects starting out in practice after school, an objective that only some will reach. If an architect is supporting a family through his or her job, with no other substantial sources of income or assets, then giving up a regular and reliable salary to venture forth as an independent practitioner can be a frightening undertaking.

Traveling and additional graduate study are other pursuits that can be extremely beneficial to an architect. They too are difficult to accomplish if one is overly encumbered with dependents, debts, or doubts. Obviously those who begin with a financial support system, or those who are personally unencumbered, have a distinct advantage. Inheriting money or being married to a working, supportive spouse helps. Likewise teaching architecture can provide both time and income for young aspiring architects to begin practices while teaching.

An architect for whom I once worked gave me some memorable advice as I was departing my summer's job to return to architectural school. Having called me into his office to say farewell, he pointed his finger toward the drafting room, then occupied by about a dozen architects bent over their drawing boards, and proposed that I should keep one thing in mind if I didn't want to "end up" like them: don't marry or have kids too soon! Of course he was really saying that if I wanted someday to travel or start a practice, too many premature commitments could stand in the way. Financial and personal obstacles can keep architects sitting in the back of drafting rooms.

Lack of Talent

Of course some people fail because they indeed lack talent. Or they don't meet all of their goals because they don't have the essential resources needed to do so. Would-be architects should consider this possibility. If some of the key intellectual and personal attributes discussed in the preceding chapter are missing, architecture can be a very uphill endeavor. Every year teachers of architecture see students who seem to be pursuing the wrong career, whose aptitudes clearly lie elsewhere. Some are uncomfortable or awkward with drawing and graphics. Others lack analytic and technical ability. Still others show little creativity, imagination, or visual sensitivity. These can be serious impediments if one desires to be an architect.

It is crucial to note that being intelligent is no guarantee of aptitude for architecture. A large dose of native talent must lie in the genes—talents can be brought forth and enhanced but not taught. Like certain personal qualities, such talent may be developed in spite of, not because of, formal education. Intuition and instinct are indispensable to architectural design; erudition and intelligence are necessary but not sufficient.

Lack of Dedication

Also indispensable to achieving in architecture are frequently extraordinary effort and dedication. Without them the prospective or practicing architect surely faces rejection and failure. Unwillingness to work hard, and to accept often minimal rewards, is a very good reason not to be an architect.

Students first discover this truism in architectural school. Being very labor intensive, requiring countless hours of mental and manual effort making drawings and crafting models, architectural study prepares one for what is to come: lots more hard work and always the potential for rejection. However, those fully committed to their work and their objectives benefit from a sort of religious sense of purpose or mission which helps them weather the rougher moments. Dedication to architecture and to work can provide a stabilizing rationale in an apparently irrational world.

Legal and Financial Risks

Architects in practice who own firms and whose designs get built are exposed to very substantial legal and financial risks. The major legal risk stems from the potential for professional negligence which can cause clients or others to suffer monetary damages. Architects are sued all the time by plaintiffs who believe that the architect negligently committed an error which caused injury or financial loss to the plaintiff. Alleged errors can include poor professional judgment, inadequate or incorrect design, acts of omission, or neglect. When such claims are made against an architect, whether groundless or not, the architect may be forced to compensate the plaintiff for some portion of the alleged damages incurred following negotiations, arbitration, or litigation. And no matter what the outcome, substantial legal fees may have to be paid.

Like others in our society who perform so-called personal services (physicians, attorneys, dentists, engineers), architects assume professional negligence liability personally, as individuals. They cannot protect their assets by incorporating. However, they can purchase insurance which, although very expensive, will cover most of the costs involved in defending and settling negligence claims.

There are several negative aspects associated with these circumstances, even with insurance. Negotiating, litigating, and settling claims is intrusive, time-consuming, and stressful. Claims and litigation are encouraged because of rising, often unrealistic expectations held by clients and consumers, leading them to sue architects even when there is little or no evidence of architectural wrongdoing. Thus the architect may be slapped with a lawsuit despite his or her innocence. Furthermore the very existence of insurance invites lawsuits. If architects were both impoverished and uninsured, they would rarely be sued.

Another unfortunate consequence of the rising tide of litigation is the increased practice of "defensive" design and excessive documentation, the creation of a "paper trail" which protects the architect against the ever-present threat of lawsuits. But this induces architects to be less innovative, to stick to the tried and true, and to devote more time to being pseudolawyers instead of designers. In any event you will eventually get sued regardless of what you do. If you want to avoid the minefield of liability and litigation, then architectural practice is unsafe ground unless you remain forever an employee.

Financially, there is an even greater risk than being sued for professional negligence, a risk mentioned earlier in this chapter and worth noting again. It's the risk of not being paid for services rendered and in turn having to take legal action to collect fees. Potentially the architect can suffer loss of income as well as time, to which may be added the stress of proving the case since, as plaintiff, the architect must assume the burden of proof. As the reader might have guessed by now, the only victors are the lawyers.

Disillusionment

All of the roadblocks, risks, and uncertainties can produce severe frustration and disillusionment, perhaps the greatest overall risk in becoming an architect. When architects have met the demands of professional preparation, paid their proverbial dues, mustered their talents, and then found their aspirations and ideals compromised, or their ideas rejected, disillusionment may be inevitable. Usually there isn't even the offsetting consolation of having made a lot of money. In fact architects say that they sometimes feel like whores, working in a profession where prostituting one's goals and standards is commonplace. A dim view indeed.

Architects periodically feel exploited or used. They sometimes provide services for little or no pay, hoping for something in the future, only to end up with nothing. Many see their career as a giant compromise, having given more than they got and accepted less than they deserved. How different, they say to themselves in retrospect, than what was imagined when they first put pencil to paper in a design studio. Some accept this condition as part of the "business" of architecture. They find sufficient rewards to offset the disappointments, or they may even be able to disregard the problems altogether. A few simply abandon the profession, seeking firmer ground.

One thing is certain. For the reader contemplating or just starting a career in architecture, there is no way to predict where the choice will lead. Undoubtedly there will be both rewards and frustrations, moments of delight and depression. The prospective architect can only hope that the sum of chapter 1's assets will exceed the sum of this chapter's liabilities, yielding a positive net worth.

II

Becoming an Architect

3

The Structure of
Architectural Education

Having reached this point, the reader should be wondering about the process of education which leads to becoming an architect. Architectural education, for many architects, is one of the most stimulating, challenging, and formative periods of their entire careers. It is also among the most frustrating and memorable, a period of trial and error, of discovery and questioning. Let's first explore the organization and structure of architectural education in the United States.

There are approximately 103 architectural schools in North America which are members of the ACSA, the Association of Collegiate Schools of Architecture. In the 1982–83 academic year there were 91 professional degree programs in the United States accredited by the NAAB, the National Architectural Accrediting Board. The NAAB periodically visits all such schools to ensure that they are meeting stipulated criteria for conducting programs in architecture. Criteria address such issues as faculty qualifications, physical facilities, budget, courses, and overall program goals. As will be seen later, these same criteria are of great interest to prospective students of architecture.

Almost all architectural schools are constituent parts of universities, existing either as departments or graduate schools within university divisions or colleges. This is appropriate because the discipline of architecture is clearly linked to many other university-based disciplines—art, engineering, physics and mathematics, history, sociology—and would suffer measurably if isolated from the academic diversity of a university. Further, courses in architecture are themselves of interest to students and faculty in other departments on university campuses.

Most states have public universities offering programs and degrees in architecture. Likewise many private universities have architectural schools. In recent years two-year community colleges have begun teaching prearchitecture courses for students planning to enroll eventually in accredited, university degree programs. There are a few, indeed very few, wholly independent schools of architecture, unaffiliated with major universities (one of the most successful of these is the Boston Architectural Center, known as the BAC, which offers a unique, accredited, cooperative program).

The appendix lists the architectural schools in existence in the United States as of 1983. It also shows the type of degree programs currently offered. Here is where the greatest confusion may arise for the prospective architectural student, for there is great variety in types of degree programs in architecture. I will try to summarize them as clearly and succinctly as possible.

Program Types

Type 1   Undergraduate, four-year programs leading to B.S. or B.A. degrees that are *not* accredited professional degrees. Many schools offer this program. After earning these degrees, students must usually spend at least two more years in a graduate program to earn an *accredited, professional degree,* in most cases a master of architecture (M.Arch.). This type of program allows students to test the waters of architecture without an excessive investment of time, in the event that they change their minds. Such preprofessional programs may provide up to half of a complete architectural curriculum.

Type 2   Undergraduate, five-year programs leading to the B.Arch. degree, which is an accredited professional degree. This used to be the norm for architectural education in the United

States, and many schools have retained this program despite the shift to graduate architectural education since the 1960s. Its advantages are less cost—five years of college versus six or seven, undergraduate tuition fees versus graduate tuition fees (almost always higher)—and academic continuity from freshman to fifth year. Its disadvantages are that it compresses both professional and general education together into an intense five-year period, often precluding exploration through elective studies in other fields; it forces an early career choice, normally at the freshman or sophomore year levels when many nineteen- or twenty-year-old students are still "questing"; and once begun, it is usually an all-or-nothing program, since the B.Arch. is available only at the end of five years.

Type 3   Graduate, professional degree programs leading to the M.Arch. for students who have already earned a B.A. or B.S. degree (type 1) in architecture. These are two- to three-year programs for those without an accredited professional degree (a B.Arch. or M.Arch.) but who hold an undergraduate degree with a major in architecture. Students in these programs enroll as graduate students, and they may hold undergraduate degrees from the same university in which they are enrolling as graduate students.

Type 4   Graduate programs leading to the first, accredited degree in architecture, usually the M.Arch. degree for students holding undergraduate degrees in majors *other* than architecture. Such programs enroll architecture students only as graduate students and normally require three to four years of intensive, graduate-level, professional studies in architecture. Students in these programs are generally assumed to have had little previous academic experience in architecture upon entering the program. Typically these programs will be populated by students with degrees in art, the humanities, engineering and science, business and economics, and the social sciences.

Type 5   Graduate programs leading to second, postprofessional degrees in architecture for students already holding B.Arch. or M.Arch. degrees. Although some Ph.D. degree programs exist, most postprofessional degree programs are at the masters level with a specific topic or area of study specified. Advanced masters degree programs in architecture may vary from one to two years in duration, depending on the school and area of study.

The lack of national consistency in programs and names of degrees results from the independent nature of individual architectural schools, coupled with the reluctance of the architectural establishment—those in practice and in education—to standardize architectural programs. For example, the NAAB, that alphabetic entity mentioned earlier which certifies architectural school programs, did not establish rigid or codified program standards until very recently. Rather, it asked schools to define their own standards and goals, and then it evaluated the success with which schools have met them. Although there are some generally accepted notions of what constitutes a legitimate architectural program, these notions permit wide latitude in designing courses and curricula. Therefore reading names of degrees and courses in catalogues reveals little of the content and specifics of a school's program.

Curricular Content

Despite the nominal variations in packaging of courses and curricula from one architectural school to another, there is nevertheless substantial commonality in content. Therefore what follows is not a description of the specific form of architectural school curricula but is rather a summary of their basic content. A

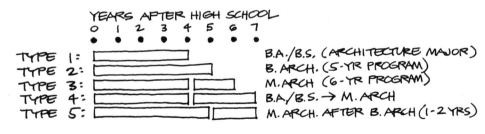

Time to complete each type of program.

course may have dozens of different names from one school to another, so it is imperative to focus on subject matter instead of labeling. Further the exact chronology of subjects offered in schools varies slightly, but again these variations are less significant than the overall sequence, which is fairly uniform.

Most school curricula require the cumulative equivalent of eight, fifteen-week semesters of architectural studies for successful completion of the professional degree program. A few graduate schools do it in six semesters. With no previous background in architecture, you should assume that most first professional degree programs will take approximately five to eight calendar years to complete after high school, depending on when you enter architectural school.

The content of architectural programs divides itself generally into three broad areas: design, history, and technology. The majority of courses in any architectural school catalog will deal explicitly with subject matter and exercises in one of these three areas, although there can be overlaps. Design necessarily considers history and technology. History of architecture is the study of the history of building and city design related to cultural, political, social, and technological history. Technology courses teach students theories and methods for carrying out architectural design concepts. This interrelation of areas of specialty is the keystone of the discipline of architecture, itself an amalgamation of disciplines.

Design

Courses in design must usually be taken in every semester or year of any architectural program. They are the unifying element, the primary pedagogical activity in school that brings together all of the diverse contributing disciplines and concerns in architecture. Design studio courses typically account for 35 to 40 percent of the total credit hours needed in architecture, and they may actually consume a disproportionately higher percentage of students' time, perhaps from 50 to 60 percent.

Integral to the study of design is the study of fundamental principles and techniques of architectural representation and composition. These include the following:

Freehand drawing   Sketching of forms, real or imagined, in two or three dimensions to develop eye-hand facility using different media (pencil primarily but also ink, charcoal, pastel, or paint) and the ability to produce sketches rapidly, comfortably, and with some accuracy; this is one of the architect's most invaluable skills.

Constructed drawing   Representing form through the mechanical construction of drawings using drafting tools—orthogonal projections (plan, elevation, section), isometric and axonometric drawing, perspective drawing (one-, two-, and three-point perspectives), and shadow projection—the most essential tools being the scale (for measuring to translate real, full-scale dimensions into proportional, scaled-down dimensions in drawings), the straightedge (a T-square or parallel bar), triangles, compass and divider, curves, erasing shield, and last, but not least, erasers.

Presentation graphics   Methods of rendering drawings and preparing presentations; the design of drawing formats and titles; selecting media and paper or board; creating washes, tones, textures, shading, and shadowing; collage; representing furniture, vegetation, people, and vehicles; the control of line weight; and the building of models.

Visual composition and analysis   Using graphic techniques and a variety of media to invent or manipulate forms in two or three dimensions, or to analyze existing forms—the objects of study can be abstract or real for purposes of inventing form, and the forms analyzed can be buildings, cities, objects, patterns, painting, sculpture—in order to discover principles of composition.

The Design Studio

The major component of the design menu is the architectural design studio where students carry out research and design for specific projects. These projects, often analogous to what architects do in practice, normally involve the design of buildings, parts of buildings, complexes of buildings, building sites, parts of cities or towns, or even entire settlements.

The architectural design studio operates fairly consistently throughout the United States. Ideally, there are from twelve to eighteen students for each design studio instructor, referred to as the studio critic, and each critic's section may be one of several at a given level within the curriculum. The studio critic may operate independently, doing his or her own projects and following his or her own schedule. Or the studio may be part of a coordinated effort involving several sections, an entire level, or even the entire school. This too can change from semester to semester within a given school.

Design studio teachers normally plan the studio course, select projects, and schedule work. Studio courses have the greatest amount of student-teacher contact in the curriculum, and more than most courses in any university. They are ordinarily six to nine credit courses (typical lecture or seminar courses are three credits) and meet three or four days per week for three to four hours per day! This means twelve to sixteen hours of in-class work and interaction weekly. Part of this time is spent working independently, part getting critiques of your work at your desk ("desk crits"), and part evaluating work in group reviews.

Generally, studio design projects increase in complexity as the student progresses through the program. Complexity depends on the number and difficulty of design issues addressed in a given project, not necessarily on a project's size or cost. A house could be a more complex project than an office building or industrial plant, depending on site conditions and design requirements. Unconstrained design problems can be far more challenging than highly constrained ones.

In well-organized programs beginning year studio projects tend to be very focused and basic, concentrating on design fundamentals. Students are introduced to concepts of spatial and functional organization, circulation, visual composition of two- and three-dimensional shapes, and structural behavior. Projects may be abstract in nature, independent of building design, to encourage abstract, creative thinking and to reinforce the graphic skills outlined earlier.

Subsequently projects become more and more like architecture, although specific requirements and conditions may still be idealized and unrealistic. Projects that illustrate this approach include small pavilions or kiosks, vacation homes or retreats (usually in the mountains or the woods, if not on the beach), small gardens, modest office buildings or simple schools. Each project may be conceived by the critic to introduce the student to new design questions while reinforcing principles already learned. One project might emphasize site planning and building massing (shaping a building's overall volume on a site), another might deal with structure, materials, and climate, and still another might focus on facades and stylistic imagery. In all proj-

A student presenting a studio design project for review by a jury.

ects the student will be concerned with the creation and manipulation of spaces, volumes, surfaces, and structures on a chosen site in response to a stipulated set of design requirements, called the project "program."

As students' competency increases, they move ahead into higher-level design studios where they explore design projects with greater depth and focus, or with more complicated and conflicting site and program requirements. Such projects include housing, health facilities, complex administrative buildings, large schools, theaters, commercial facilities, libraries, museums, transportation terminals, or office towers. More sophisticated site planning occurs, and some projects entail the design of neighborhoods, city blocks, streetscapes, town or city centers, transportation corridors, public parks, and subdivisions.

The last semester of design frequently involves a thesis. This may require research and preparation in the preceding semester, during which the student selects a topic or project and gathers the data needed to undertake the design. Most thesis work is done independently, unlike the preceding design studios (where students work together and see their instructors two or three times per week). Thesis students normally have an adviser or advisory committee of faculty who may review the student's progress only four or five times before the final presentation. Also some schools require submission of a written thesis document, especially at the master's level, which must include photoreductions of all drawings and models produced.

Almost all architectural schools have adopted minimum standards of competency and performance which students must meet before advancing to the next level of design studio, or before graduation. Since the design studio sequence is continuous throughout most programs, it is not unusual to find studio sections with students who did not all begin architectural school at the same time. Many take extra time to complete architectural school for academic and personal reasons (such as finances), so don't be surprised to find this kind of population mix in studio courses.

History

History, the second broad area of study within any architectural program, is concerned with the past, but also impinges on the present and future. By studying history, the prospective architect learns the who, what, when, where, how, and why of what has gone before. Looking back, however, also discloses ideas, beliefs, theories, and practices that may be relevant to what architects do today or tomorrow. The study of history introduces the architect to his or her legacy and suggests how that legacy might be applicable to the future.

History of architecture may be approached chronologically, geographically, and topically. In other words, the historian may consider the development of architecture by time periods (decades, centuries, or eras), by location (cities, regions, countries, or continents), or by specific topics of interest (focusing on styles, architects, technology, symbology, philosophy, building types, for example). Each historian in each school will have his or her own special way of thinking about and presenting architectural history, but there is again substantial commonality in content. Following is a representative, though inevitably incomplete, list of course content in architectural history:

Surveys of western architectural history from ancient to modern (usually fast, focusing on slide images and major historical periods).

Surveys of nonwestern architectural history, primarily Islamic and far eastern cultures (much rarer than western history).

Ancient western architectural history, concentrating on Egypt, the near east, Greece, and Rome.

Early Christian and Byzantine architecture.

Architecture of the middle ages, primarily the Gothic in France, Italy, and England.

The Renaissance, primarily Italy.

Architectural history between the Renaissance and the industrial revolution—the Baroque and Rococo periods in Europe, Neoclassicism in France and England.

The French Beaux Arts influence from the eighteenth to the twentieth century.

American architecture in the nineteenth and twentieth centuries.

Modern and post modern American architecture.

Modern European architecture, usually divided into pre-WW I, between the wars, and post-WW II periods.

History of Russian architecture.

History of Japanese architecture.

History of indigenous architectures (usually across diverse regional, cultural, temporal, and technological lines).

History of Islamic architecture.

History of architectural theory.

History of building technology.

History of landscape architecture.

History of urban design, exploring the form and origins of towns, cities, and urban spaces.

No one school covers all of these in its collection of history courses, and no student can begin to study but a fraction of the topics on this list. The survey courses first listed, lasting one or two semesters, skim the surface of the past, whereas smaller lecture or seminar courses provide the opportunity to concentrate on the subsequently listed topics. Once in school you will quickly uncover your interests and learn which teachers and courses appeal to you.

Like related courses in the humanities, history courses in architectural school consist of assigned and recommended reading, coupled with the extensive viewing of slides selected and projected by the lecturer or seminar leader (who may at times be a student in the class). Essays, term papers, and small projects are usually assigned. Depending on the school's location and resources, teachers may lead students on field trips. Indeed, field trips are popular in studio and technology courses as well.

Technology

Technology categorizes the third type of architectural course work found in all professional school curricula. Broad and encompassing, it refers to those subjects dealing with how designs are implemented, with principles and methods of construction and environmental control. It should not be thought of as somehow separate and different from *design*, however. Instead, it allows us to label easily those courses which are more closely associated with science, engineering, and management, as to both content and method.

Within the sphere of architectural technology there are four subtechnologies: structural technology, construction materials and methods, environmental control technology, and management or business technology. Some of each is required in all architectural schools, although in differing doses and with widely ranging levels of rigor. Further, like design and history, the subjects of architectural technology are included in the examinations given by states for the licensing of architects. And the essential subject matter in architectural technology is more easily understood by aspiring architects who have some knowledge of mathematics and physics, a reason many schools require beginning students to take introductory calculus and physics.

Structures

The study of structural concepts is indispensable for anyone who hopes to design and build buildings. "Structure" is that part of a building, or any constructed form, which provides support. The structure resists the loads of gravity (weight), wind, earth movement, and other forces that may be applied to the structure at any time. Some of these loads act vertically, such as gravity, and some horizontally or laterally, such as wind or earthquake forces. Architects also refer to the structure of a building as the building skeleton or frame, and in certain structures, walls, floors, and roofs constitute integral elements of the framing system. Any element that contributes to the stability of a structure under conditions of loading becomes a member of the structural frame or system.

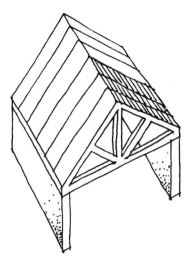

Obviously many components of a building are not part of the building's structural system—its plumbing or its windows, for example. Not so obvious, however, is the role that the structural system plays in affecting, or being affected by, the overall spatial and volumetric form of a building. First, the structure must be designed to work safely and efficiently in supporting and stabilizing the building. Second, the architect must orchestrate both the patterns of framing and the patterns of architectural form (volume, space, surface) to create visual and constructional relationships. Here is clearly the interface between the technology of structure and the art of design.

To master this, students in architectural school study statics (forces on bodies in equilibrium) and the strengths of materials (how materials behave under stress), and the behavior of fundamental structural components—beams, columns, cables, rods, footings and foundations, bearing walls, and slabs or decks—when forces are applied to them. They learn about stresses and strains, deflection, bending, buckling, tension and compression, all of which occur when elements of a structure are loaded. They also learn about connections and joints between members, about temperature expansion and contraction, and about entire structural systems (for example, how entire building frames behave when loaded). Such systems include the familiar balloon frame of a house, post and beam framing typical of office buildings, bearing wall construction, membrane or tensile structures (such as tents or bridges), thin shell structures (plates, vaults, domes), trusses, space frames, and others.

Do not suppose, at this point, that the architect is expected to practice engineering, to design in detail the structure of buildings he or she designs. You will not be able to do so in most cases, even if you wanted to. Architects in practice rely on structural engineers for the specific design of all load-bearing components of buildings. But the architect must know the fundamentals, be able to guide and understand the engineer's work, and contribute directly to the decision making which determines the look, quality, and cost of a structural system.

Materials and Methods of Construction

Beyond structural systems architects must know the implications of using the primary structural materials: wood, steel, and concrete. Each material has unique characteristics, both structurally and aesthetically, and the architect must choose materials and systems thoughtfully and knowledgeably. Strength, durability, workability, weight, resistance to heat and weather, and cost are among the properties considered. In school students may also be introduced to other materials as well—plastics, glass, fibers, metals other than steel, and composites.

Although it is common practice to rely on structural engineers for the final design of structural systems, the architect retains primary responsibility for determining and designing the details of assembly of building components. Some schools teach theory and practice of detailed design (detailing) in specialized courses which develop knowledge about the performance of materials and manufactured components. Here the designer is concerned with the control of moisture, heat loss and gain, dimensional stability, durability, availability of labor and materials, cost, and last but not least, appearance. The architect must show in design drawings how pieces fit together, how joints and connections are made, and what the dimensions of all assembled components will be. Typical details depict roof, wall, and floor assemblies, window and door assemblies, railings, stairs, cabinetry, and decorative finishing elements.

Environmental Controls

Studies in environmental control technology are concerned with making the built environment comfortable and usable for human occupancy. They are also concerned with the use and conservation of energy within buildings. With the help of engineering specialists, architects must fashion ambient environments that are safe from fire, offer thermal comfort (neither too cold or too hot), are properly lighted, provide fresh air to breathe, and have appropriate acoustic characteristics. In an era of expensive and curtailed supplies of energy, buildings must be designed that are well insulated, retaining heat and capturing the sun's energy in winter and rejecting it in summer.

In addition to tempering the environment and satisfying the senses, architects and their consultants must design systems for distributing energy, fluids, gases, goods and people within buildings. These systems are like metabolic networks woven into the rigid, supporting skeleton of a building's body. Students of architecture study the basics of electrical systems, plumbing systems, heating and cooling systems, ventilating systems, and conveying systems (elevators and escalators). They learn both engineering principles and specific applications, understanding how such systems influence overall building design. As with structural systems architectural designers generally do not undertake the detailed, quantitative design of environmental control systems but rather collaborate with engineering experts in system selection and design coordination.

Many schools offer courses that cover lighting, both natural and artificial, and acoustics. Students may study room acoustics, the behavior and perception of sound within spaces, and sound transmission, the passage of sound between spaces or through structures. Anyone who has functioning eyes and ears knows that the world is full of architecture where sight and sound are difficult, if not impossible.

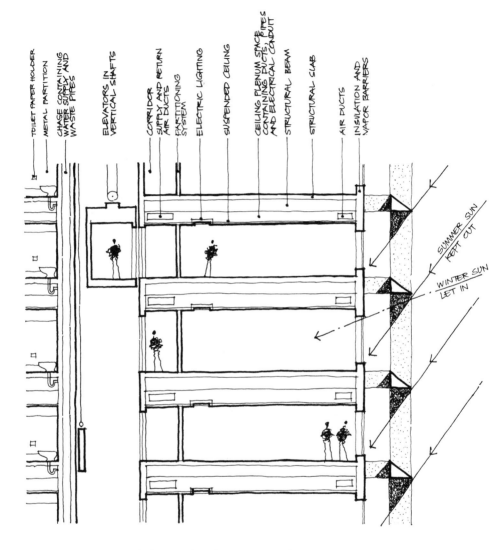

Some of the systems and elements that shape, serve, and
control buildings and the spaces within.

Management

Management, the fourth subtopic under technology, is somewhat of a catchall. It embraces those topics and courses that prepare students to conduct the business affairs and operational tasks of architecture. Included are courses that address business administration, methods of practice, finance and economics, legal concerns, and construction management. Schools vary greatly in the number and variety of such courses taught, with some offering very few. They may rely on courses given in other departments (business administration, economics, computer science, or civil engineering) to satisfy students' needs and interests.

Almost all architectural schools teach at least one course about professional architectural practice. These courses explain how firms are organized and managed. They delve into marketing of services, fees and compensation, project management and documentation, contracts, legal and ethical concerns, and construction administration. More advanced courses focused on the management of construction projects are beginning to appear in architectural schools. These deal with planning and scheduling of construction tasks, coordination of building trades and subcontractors, estimating and bidding, materials purchasing, contract negotiating, and cost accounting. However, many schools of architecture have resisted introducing this subject matter which, to some, appears to be invading the territory of the general contractor. They would argue that construction management belongs more appropriately in schools of management or engineering.

Several schools teach real estate economics. Such courses may examine the sources of capital for building, the development process through which buildings are created, the economic characteristics of projects built in both the private and public sectors, and the role of government in architecture—its regulations, zoning and building codes, tax and investment laws, planning policy, and construction programs.

The computer is now here to stay. It is rapidly becoming an everyday tool in design, management, and production, and architecture is no exception. A number of architectural schools have been heavily committed since the 1960s to research and development in the field of computer-aided design and computer graphics. Other schools require or encourage their students to take at least an introductory course in the theory and use of computers.

Sophisticated computer systems are now available for architectural firms at reasonable prices, systems that can draw complex designs on both video displays and paper, some in color. These same machines do other things beside acting as draftspersons. They can be used to write reports or specifications, process and store data, print charts and diagrams, and handle accounting. There is little doubt that computers will continue to become smaller, faster, more capable, easier to use, and cheaper. Therefore it seems inevitable that more and more architectural school programs will be obliged to let the computer in and to exploit it for the valuable tool that it is.

Electives

Courses in design, history, and technology are the core of an architectural curriculum, but that core should be complemented by electives in other areas of study. Indeed, electives may be required. They broaden professional education and may furnish credit hours needed for graduation. Some architectural courses, particularly in history or technology, can be taken as electives when they are not part of the core requirements. Electives outside of architecture may offer the largest and most fertile selection, however, reinforcing the liberal-professional duality of architectural education.

Following are courses or topics most relevant to the study and practice of architecture. Again, the list is inevitably incomplete.

Urban planning

Geography

Horticulture and landscape architecture

Anthropology and archaeology

Art

Sociology

Psychology

Economics

Business administration and management science

Civil engineering

History

Government and politics

The foregoing discussion of curricular content should make clear why schools of architecture are integral constituents of universities, in contrast to law or medical schools. The latter, though attached to universities, tend to operate independently, with little academic interaction between the professional school and the rest of the university community. Nevertheless, architectural schools do develop their own, conspicuous, iconoclastic identities within the university setting. Likewise architectural school applicants and students must create their own identities, and the following chapters will suggest how the identities of both individuals and institutions are measured.

4

Experiencing Architectural School

If the previous chapter succeeded in outlining the structure and protocols of architectural education in the United States, it in no way conveyed the feeling, the experience, the sensations of being an architectural student. They constitute a kind of road map for a journey, not the journey itself. Somewhere between the journey experience and the road map, there might be something—perhaps like a documentary film or detailed diary—that is less than the journey but more than the road map. This chapter will, I hope, be such an account, the next best thing to being there.

The First Year and Work Load Shock

The first year of immersion in architectural school is an encounter, a mystery, and a surprise. No matter how well prepared you are or what you have been told, it will be different from what you expected. The real first year is that year when you are enrolled in the beginning studio design courses while taking other architectural courses as well. You will be very, very busy.

In fact one of the first shocks is how busy you will be, the work load shock. Few students, either from high school or college, anticipate the amount of work piled on in architectural school, especially the first year. It seems to be a tradition, one of many, for the first-year introductory design studio to set the initial pace. That pace is incredibly hectic and intense. It involves steady, unending assignments of variable duration. Some require hours, some days, whereas others last weeks (often broken down into shorter subassignments). The stoccato rhythm of basic design projects demands constant effort, day and night at times, far beyond the credit hour allotment that catalogs cite.

The work load shock, like any assault on the mind and body, produces both positive and negative responses. Negatively, it is tiring, enervating, numbing. Much of the studio work is labor intensive rather than intellect intensive. Hours are spent drawing or crafting things. Some of these hours will seem tedious and others exhilarating. Up moments are later wiped out by down moments as the continuous struggle to keep going and keep abreast, let alone ahead, goes on. Second winds, bursts of adrenalin, and moments of great strength recur with reasonable frequency. If you can tolerate it all, it will toughen you for things to come.

Part of coping with work load shock is time management. With the design studio demanding so much time and energy, how does one meet other obligations? There seems to be a deadline every other day and some days two or three. Lulls are few and far between. The faculty will usually tell you that you should simply try to work steadily and regularly in each subject, to allocate your time to each course continuously throughout the semester. Easier said than done.

Much of the work is produced in intense spurts, usually just before the deadlines. Somehow the creative process appears to defy attempts at smoothness and continuity and regularity. Architects refer to such spurts as "charrettes." The charrette, a French word meaning little cart, applies to any intense, uninterrupted period of work prior to a deadline, almost always including at least one all-night stand (many years ago, at the Ecole des Beaux Arts in Paris, as students frantically completed their last-minute work, a "charrette" would arrive to collect their drawings just prior to the final deadline). If you visit an architectural school studio today, ideally near the end of a semester, you will see students "on charrette" day and night. Many never go home. Some practically live in the studio in what can best be described as camping-out conditions.

The only attitude that makes sense for handling first-year work loads is a positive, have fun, on-to-victory one. *Illegitimus non carborundum*, interpreted liberally to mean "don't let the bastards grind you down!" Hang in, be tough, enjoy the pain and the degradation as well as the successes and the enlightenment. Amaze your friends and family with your dedication and suffering. Other students in the university will be awed by your commitment and endurance. Rare is the campus where the architecture students are not considered the most hardworking, grind-it-out students or where architecture is not considered one of the hardest majors.

You will find little sympathy among most faculty when you air your complaints about the amount of work you have to do, the overlapping deadlines and exams, the pressures, and the state of your deteriorating health. Their lack of sympathy does not mean that they do not understand or appreciate your plight. They've been through it too. They know that you are behind in sleep, neglecting your friends or family, in desperate need of a bath, and probably going broke while trying to pay your way through school. They know that your love life is suffering or interfering with your work. But they will tell you it's inevitable, a simulation of the real world. It's part of the rites of passage, like so many others a deposit on account of the dues one must pay to become an architect. The work load and its pressures are a positive stimulus as well as an ordeal.

New Values, New Language

The work load shock is accompanied by the value and language shocks. The latter results from being suddenly deluged by a new vocabulary. It is also an imprecise vocabulary. Only architects and a few architectural groupies really know the lingo. Indeed, there are sublingos which are accessible only to a minority of architects. You will first hear the language from your teachers, then from upper-level students and others who read the architectural media and architectural books.

Value shock is related to language shock because values are professed most frequently through language. To appreciate value shock, you must accept the notion, a priori, that all academic or professional fields have elaborately developed, internal value systems. A value system is a set of commonly understood criteria or standards by which people and their work are measured within the field. This set of values and criteria, like its concomitant vocabulary, is not clearly written down anywhere. You can't go out and buy a book titled "Architecture's Value System: How to Judge Everything You See or Hear" or one on "Words Architects Use and What They Mean."

The values and vocabulary of architecture in school come as a shock because, first, they are unfamiliar; second, they are unclear and ambiguous; and third, their application changes from person to person or week to week. Just when you thought you had begun to figure out what your teacher was talking about, new data arrive and renew your confusion. Let's focus on some of these values and use of language.

Architecture is at once an art and a science. It demands logic, method, rational analysis, and measurable quantification, on one hand, and intuition, emotion, sentiment, willfulness, and subjective judgment, on the other. Thus the beginning student immediately faces continual conflict and uncertainty. Values and judgments that cannot possibly be justified scientifically are presented, primarily in the design studio.

But the teacher insists on work that is both reasonable and aesthetically satisfying, if not innovative and newsworthy. Since most architecture students share traditional secondary and college academic experiences, they share similar expectations when they embark on a new subject in a new course: the teacher presents specific material, asks specific questions, with the student periodically regurgitating, often with minimum digestion, what has been presented. Emphasis was always on finding answers, on deriving solutions. The student longs to know what the teacher "wants." "Tell us!" say the students, "and we'll give it to you."

Yet the values espoused by studio critics may seem vague, the pedagogical expectations ill-defined. One day, the critic says that it is important to think about efficient and legible circulation, and the next day the critic protests that your design is too much like a circulation diagram. Too little color one day, too much the next. Nice proportions, proclaims the critic, but it doesn't work; it works, but the proportions are bad. Be simple, they say. Too simpleminded, they say. It has wonderful complexity . . . it's too complex . . . it lacks complexity. Less is more. You can't read the structure. Why express the structure? Too much variety! Too little variety!

Perhaps the intertwining of values and vocabulary is becoming apparent. What about these words which teachers utter so often, so confidently, so critically? What do they mean, and what do the teachers really want? How do they, much less beginning students, know when a proportion is bad, or which colors to use, or when there is just the right amount of complexity. Obviously, claim the students, the critics know something—some set of understood but not explicitly communicated values—which allows them to make judgments and to know the truth. Why not share it?

Words expressing the values pour forth. Buildings are described as "constructs," "environments," "environmental domains," "built form," "structures." The word "space" can refer to a room, a corridor or hallway, a street, a plaza, an attic, an interval, or any void. Space can "flow," "penetrate," "articulate," "modulate," "expand," or "contract." Space can be amorphous and open, or crisply defined and contained. A closet or bathroom is a space, and the mall in Washington, D.C., or New York's Central Park is a space.

Building components familiar to everyone are favorites for renaming. Windows become "fenestration," "voids" in walls, "oculi," "penetrations," "openings," "apertures," or "cutouts." Walls become vertical "planes," "membranes," "surfaces," "space definers or delimiters," "enclosing envelopes," "partitions," or "separators." A courtyard may be an "atrium," a "peristyle," or an "interior open space," whereas a porch translates into a "loggia," a "portico," or a "transitional space." Corridors are called "galleries," "circulation conduits," "pedestrian streets," "passages," "channels," "ambulatories," and, occasionally, "hallways."

Critics and students like to talk about the visual characteristics of form. Representative of some of the nouns and adjectives one hears are the following:

Scale   Having to do with the relative sizes of the whole and its constituent parts, and in turn their relation to human dimensions

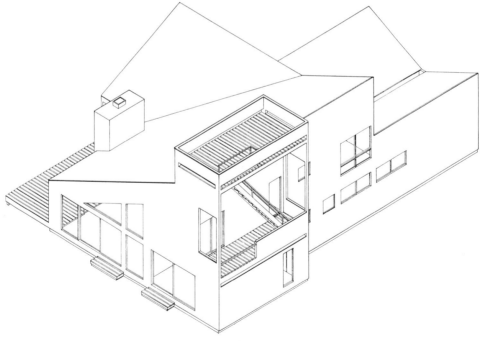

Axonometric drawing of a vacation house; note windows
(fenestration, voids, penetrations, cutouts) in exterior walls
(vertical planes, surfaces, envelopes, membranes).

Appropriateness   Whether a design "fits" the circumstances defining the project.

Image   Concerned with the "look" of things—their general appearance, character, and style.

Texture, shape, rhythm, relief, color, dimension   Pseudo-objectifiable visual qualities applicable to any architectural form.

Metaphor   A popular term used to denote the ability of architecture to look or be like something else—buildings as "machines," living "organisms," geometric solids (cubes, spheres, rectangular "slabs" or "bars," cylinders, lattices, pyramids, chains, mats, or combinations of these), or other human-made constructions (including such things as appliances, tools, furniture, bridges, containers, musical instruments, and works of art).

Function   Presumed to refer to the way in which architecture fulfills objectifiable requirements relating to utility and usefulness, structural stability, human comfort and safety, buildability, and cost (the presumption is that functional considerations are different than aesthetic ones in that they are rational, somewhat quantifiable, and free of ego influence).

Form, formal, formalistic   Very broad terms that relate to the physical, three-dimensional, distinctly visual nature and shape of those things designed or studied by architects (objects, spaces, structural elements, ornaments, cities, and plants all have "form" and "formal/formalistic" qualities).

Circulation   Often-used word describing the "form," pattern, and method of movement within or through an environment—circulation of people, vehicles, and goods horizontally and vertically in buildings, cities, rooms, or landscapes.

Unity, harmony, coherence   Denoting, in any composition, that quality whereby the whole and its parts somehow belong together through visual linkages or interrelationships, of which there can be many (dependent on the eye of the beholder).

Disunity, incoherence, fragmentation   The opposite of the preceding values, also dependent on individual perception (one person's harmony may be another's incoherence).

Friedrich Schinkel's early nineteenth century perspective drawing of a theater for Berlin; note that the building is a composition of rectangular and cylindrical forms layered horizontally and vertically, unified by repetition of elements and continuous bands of ornamentation, and given scale by such recognizable features as stair risers and windows in the rusticated stone base.

Layering and layers The perception of multiple elements—walls, lines of columns, doors or windows, roofs, ornamentation—distributed in space so that the observer sees several at one time proceeding from foreground to background, from front to back or top to bottom (if you look down a city street, you will see "layers" of buildings lining the street, "layers" of signs and columns and storefronts and sidewalk elements including trees, benches, parking meters).

It reads Meaning that a design intent can be seen, stands out, and/or can be interpreted ("read" like a book or a facial expression); examples of reading buildings can include the reading of patterns, of entries and doorways, of functions within, of materials and structure, of symbolic content (think of Gothic cathedrals or the New York Stock Exchange)—and if it can't be read, according to the critic, then you may have to "rewrite."

There are hundreds of adjectives that season the comments and critiques of architects, especially when making remarks about students' work. A few are heard often:

Interesting A word that may mean anything from boring, banal, passable, or conventional to provocative, inventive, stimulating, or witty—an "interesting" design is rarely an A, whereas "very interesting" may be in the A category.

Competent Like "interesting" may imply that a design is merely okay, workable, acceptable, but certainly not brilliant or revolutionary—competent is what every architect is expected to be at a minimum.

Convincing Cropping up regularly, means that some specific design appears to be well thought out *and* well executed in the drawings or model of the design—"convincing" says that you have created something that is believable both artistically and functionally.

Ugly Yes, ugly is heard frequently and needs little explanation, except it really means that the critic doesn't like the looks of what you have designed, for whatever reasons—which he or she may never elaborate on—whereas others may instead find your design . . .

Beautiful Of course means that they like the looks of your design, also for reasons that may not always be clear—remember that in architecture, like all art, beauty is in the eye of the beholder!

Meaningful and meaningless Have to do with what designs "say," represent, stand for, denote, and connote, rather than what they actually do or look like—columns *are* vertical structural elements that support loads and play a role in a building's composition, but they could also *have* meaning, standing for such things as virility, continuity, verticality, trees, victory, connection from heaven to earth, or any other "idea" advocated by their designer or by historians—and for some teachers and architects, designs that cannot be thusly read or interpreted are therefore "meaningless," as may be the word "meaningful."

Throughout this book the reader will encounter much more of the architect's vocabulary. But this is only the proverbial tip of the iceberg. Perhaps it is the uncertainty and subjectivity of architectural values that lead us to search so relentlessly for a pseudoscientific language, for a new set of words and definitions every year. And every year, with each new batch of jargon and classifiers, the list of vocabulary lengthens, while the uncertainty and subjectivity continue to exist as always. Thus the beginning architectural student should know that this is itself part of the tradition and should not let first-year mumbo jumbo deter the quest for creative solutions, enlightenment, and rationality.

Competition and Grades

It is common knowledge in architectural school that many who start never finish. As chapter 2 explained, there are many reasons for people dropping out, the work load and competition being among them. However, few quit simply because of the amount of work, to which most quickly become accustomed. On the other hand, there is a keen and discernable atmosphere of competition, intensified by the artistic nature of the work in design studio, and this atmosphere can discourage even the most hardworking.

Naturally most institutions use grades to indicate how students are doing with respect to the competition within the class or school. This is certainly not unique to architecture. What is unique is that diligence and hard work do not necessarily bring correspondingly high grades. In fact another of the great first-year shocks may occur when a project you have designed with all of the blood, sweat, tears, time, and imagination you could summon gets "shot down," panned, judged a failure. And this can happen inconsistently and without warning. You may have received an A or B on your last project, then a C, D, or F on the next one. What does one make of this?

First, it is all normal. Your work, not you, is what's judged. Remember that most students experience the roller coaster of project grading throughout school. But it takes getting used to. Many students have both good and bad semesters, good and bad months, weeks or days. Keep reminding yourself that effort alone is not being assessed in architecture school, that native aptitude and talent are essential and dominant factors.

Second, most faculty grade students' work in architectural design both on a curve (that is, relative to only those students in a section or class) and against some general set of standards applied to all students. Occasionally every project in a section fails or, conversely, earns an A or B. Semesters occur during which no one receives an A, and others when nearly everyone receives an A. This depends on the critic as well as the students.

You must be philosophical about grading, recognizing that grades *only* represent the combined objective *and* subjective evaluation of your work at a particular time. They may change as you proceed through school and as your work changes. They neither destroy nor ensure your future career. Once out of architectural school, it is probable that no one will ever again see or care about your grades as a student. But one thing is certain—if you don't make the effort and do the work, you will not receive good grades, no matter how gifted you are.

The competition in architectural school is typical of grade competition anywhere. Once admitted, you are expected to maintain some minimum grade point average for continuation in the program. Most graduate schools require a minimum grade point average (GPA) of B (3.0) for graduation. Also many programs will not allow architecture students to proceed to the next level of design studio with less than adequate performance in design, even if their GPA's are high enough. Therefore students feel pressured by the need to maintain their academic standing, but this is usually a problem for a minority of students in a class.

More stressful and motivating is the pressure of wanting to excel, to stand out, to be on top, or at least near it. This is a competitive pressure whose sources are both internal and external. The dedicated student will push himself or herself, notwithstanding other influences, reacting to an internal need to achieve. With this comes pushing from external sources, which can be relentless and unending—faculty, fellow students, friends and family. Again some students thrive on such pressures, while others experience substantial stress and anxiety which can affect their work. The pressures are there, the competition and pushing are inevitable, and you must at least cope with them. Ideally they will cause you to do your best and succeed, happily.

Pencilphobia

Pencil and paper are to the architect as violin and bow are to the violinist. Like the violinist the architect must practice design (not drafting) hour after hour with pencil and paper, years of repetition to produce the music of design. Architects must become so comfortable and facile with their instruments that they can engage in the act of design only with pencil in hand. In designing architecture, the hand, pencil, and mind are merged; they act together, as one.

Drawing entails expressing graphic hypotheses, making proposals and decisions on paper, and many architecture students discover this painfully. They develop a fear of committing themselves and their ideas to paper, a fear of drawing, albeit an unconscious fear. The reluctance to draw stems from anxiety and, again, uncertainty. The beginning student quickly learns that without a drawing to look at, the critic assumes that there is no design yet, nothing tangible to evaluate. In the design studio many teachers will refuse to discuss students' design proposals or ideas unless they have been drawn. At the same time students can also discover that these same teachers may make what seem to be exclusively negative comments when the indispensable drawings are presented. So it is not unusual for some students to acquire pencilphobia as a defense, a way of avoiding the risk of failing, of being criticized.

Architectural design is a process which is inherently one of *trial* and *error*. You must use drawings as the primary method to hypothesize (to try) a design and the evaluation of drawn designs to refine and perfect them through the discovery and purging of errors. Design is a continuous trial-test-change process. Without this iteration of using pencil and paper (and often models) you will not go far as an architectural designer. Therefore draw freely, willingly, and accurately. More design study sketches are always better than less. Twenty minutes of thoughtful criticism, even if disapproving, is far more valuable than two minutes of verbal lamentations and regrets.

The Jury System

No tradition is as tenacious and enduring as the architectural school jury review. The jury review marks the end of work on a design project, or project phase, when the students present their finished drawings and models for evaluation by an assembled group of critics, the esteemed "jury." Most juries are composed of the studio critic, other invited faculty, and outside guests who may be architects or hypothetical clients. Although jury reviews are sometimes closed to the students and public, this method of review has almost disappeared. The jury review is seen as a very significant educational experience and therefore is almost always open to all, with students participating and listening from beginning to end, including students from other studios.

The typical jury protocol involves students hanging their work on the wall and, at their turn, standing in front of their drawings or model, all eyes upon them, while making an oral presentation of their project to the jury. Ideally the graphic presentation should speak for itself, but the student is allowed to sell his or her concept with words as well and subsequently to defend it. This sounds simple and reasonable, but it is not an educational experience familiar to most students prior to arriving in architectural school. Thus one cannot appreciate the jury experience without some specific observations.

You must first imagine yourself as the student preparing for the jury. Two concerns preoccupy every waking moment: (1) will you have a complete presentation with drawings and model both readable and finished; (2) will your design be praised or ridiculed by the jury. These are separate though related concerns.

Satisfactorily completing work depends on the ability to manage time, organize tasks, make decisions, and draw. You quickly learn in the first year of school that it's a great sin to pin up an incomplete presentation for the jury's consumption. The jurors, usually from three to eight in number, will amost always cite students whose work is unfinished, vaguely described, or unreadable, regardless of the merits of the students' creative or conceptual thinking. Sometimes, jurors will refuse to review incomplete presentations, especially if the student attempts to fill in the gaps verbally. Typically jurors chastise the beleaguered student, expressing dismay, disappointment, or even anger.

Jurors who believe in positive reinforcement might say: "This could have been a great scheme, if only we could have seen it all," or "One more week and this would be smashing," or "It's a shame that your presentation doesn't do justice to your idea," or "What we see only suggests its potential quality."

Jurors believing in negative reinforcement might say: "You certainly had enough time to finish this project," or "How can you ask us to review so flimsy a presentation?" or "You're never going to make it with presentations like this," or "Why do you expect us to waste our time on incomplete work?" or "The least we expect is completion of the *minimum* required drawings."

Often jurors lace their remarks with humor and sympathy, but just as often with sarcasm and disdain. In anticipation or even fear of being on the receiving end of such attacks, students mount heroic efforts to be or to appear complete when the final deadline arrives. But students vary considerably in their ability to pace themselves, to budget time, and to produce drawings and models. Some finish with ease, while others must struggle to finish.

However, the other preoccupation before each jury concerns the project itself. Will the proposed design be marginally acceptable? competent? perhaps good? maybe even outstanding? Since the question of quality is one of judgment in the eyes of the jurors, it is a relative preoccupation. You may love your design, and your design critic may love it, but the jury might not.

Anticipating a jury's response to your project is impossible. Further, anxiety about the jury's response is intensified because of the tremendous investment of effort, thought, and creative energy made prior to the jury. You say to yourself, "That's not just my work hanging up there, that's me!" A criticism of your design is interpreted by your ego as a criticism of you personally. Either consciously or subconsciously, you think, "If they don't like my work, then they don't like *me!*"

Telling you that this is not true, that jurors are evaluating your work, not you as a person, is no guarantee that such feelings will disappear. You know that you will feel good if the jury seems to like your work and bad if they don't, hence the anxiety.

Another factor contributes to jury jitters for many students—the jury limelight, the public nature of it all. There they are, faculty and students, professionals and peers, staring at you and your presentation, waiting to see if you succeed or fail. The blood rushes, palms sweat, mouth dries, the words you intended pronouncing never come forth. You worry about appearing foolish, showing anger or embarrassment, crying, arguing insultingly with a juror who has maligned your efforts. For some students mundane and insignificant preoccupations may intrude upon consciousness under the pressure of standing before a jury, life on the line. "How do I look? fly open? do I smell?" After a charrette these concerns may be justifiable.

For many students, anticipating the jury is exhilarating. It's a kind of show and tell, sometimes a game of one-upmanship. Such students are usually self-confident, no matter what the quality of their work, and relish the challenge of the jury review and the opportunity to show their stuff. It can be an ego trip if you believe in yourself and your work, even in the face of negative criticism. Those with gambling, risk-taking instincts welcome the unpredictability of the jury, hoping to win while knowing that there is always a chance of losing.

No description of the jury system would be complete without portraying the behavioral characteristics of jurors, what they do and say, and how they interact with students and with each other. Assessing architectural design is a subjective, taste-dependent process, so that each juror brings to the review his or her own particular interests, opinions, prejudices, and idiosyncracies. Students in a jury commonly hear remarks made by jurors that seem vague, unclear, confusing, contradictory, needlessly deprecating, self-laudatory, or irrelevant. Especially amusing, though sometimes confusing to the student being reviewed, can be debates between jurors. The debate may begin over the student's work, but frequently it progresses into a more general disagreement over opposing polemics or conflicting values. Such debates can also be very enlightening to those students awake and listening, for the arguments always apply to projects other than the one on the wall.

Some jurors are relatively silent and passive, saving their remarks for propitious moments, or comment on only the weightiest of issues. Jurors intimidate each other, depending on interpersonal chemistry. Some are very talkative and demonstrative, seizing every opening to take the floor. Others pontificate about the world of architecture and human condition. Jurors may say little that is specific about the work on the wall or they may offer very detailed, specific criticism of the student's design.

Some jurors dominate the jury due to their verbal wit, professional prominence, personal charisma, or persistent intervention. Still others specialize, talking only about one aspect of architectural design—site planning or structure or solar energy or formal composition—to the exclusion of other aspects. Eventually students get to know the faculty well enough to predict what they will focus on, although they can rarely predict their reactions.

After the review students may not know whether the jurors approved or disapproved, whether the jury comments were positive or negative. This results from hearing both praise and criticism at the same time, hearing that this is good while that is bad. The students wonder what silence on the part of a juror means, and they cringe whenever the word "but . . ." rings out. Some jurors sketch directly on students' drawings to make their point or illustrate an idea. If they are thoughtful, they do it in pencil, although such sketches in ink or grease pencil may make a more indelible impression. Students strain to interpret jurors' implicit reactions, their demeanor, facial expressions, body movements, and inaudible utterances. Jurors cover their mouths and chins, scratch their heads or cheeks, lean precariously forward in their chairs, get up and walk around while studiously eyeing the drawings or model. They continually whisper to one another or pass notes. What are they thinking? Is it plus or minus?

The confusion may be compounded when, hours or days after the jury, the student learns that the jurors thought highly of the project whereas the student's impression was the opposite. Having believed the jury review a disaster and feeling discouraged, the student is pleasantly surprised when the studio critic conveys the good news. Likewise the opposite occurs. The student senses that the jury went well, or remembers only positive comments, and then, after the ensuing period of elation and pride, learns that the jurors thought the work, on the whole, quite mediocre. Of course individual jurors do not always agree as to the quality of student work, and it is not unusual to receive an A or B from one while another dispenses a C or D. However, most jury grades cluster.

A few architectural students and teachers question the value of the traditional jury as a pedagogical device. They argue that it is excessively time-consuming—juries can easily last five or six hours, depending on the size of the class and number of jurors (more jurors means more time)—and too frequently degrading to students. They claim that juries are repetitious, with the same comments heard over and over again. To them, juries are boring and destructive, self-indulgent word games for faculty which serve only to put down the students. Also some argue that the jury process places undue emphasis on presentation graphics at the expense of design content and conceptual quality.

Although some of these criticisms are well founded, the jury system nevertheless survives because it achieves results that would be otherwise impossible to obtain: it simulates to some extent the reality of making presentations in practice; it reinforces the importance of meeting deadlines; it provides a forum for students to see each other's work and for faculty to see the work of students other than their own; it encourages graphic quality; and through jury discussion, it raises important issues and promotes new thinking. Like it or not, the architectural jury is probably here to stay and represents one of the unique, recurring experiences in architectural education. It is, after all, the ceremonial culmination of each studio design project, the place where all of the skills, knowledge, and ideas of the prospective architect must fuse and find expression. In judging design, it celebrates design and the art of architecture.

Other Traditions

As you might guess from reading about studio courses and juries, design activity dominates other course work and activities in most architectural schools. At times the demands of the studio, coupled with poor time management by students, totally eclipse the performance of other duties. Teachers of history or technology courses can count on extensive absenteeism just prior to scheduled design studio deadlines and juries, particularly at the end of each semester. Or they know that, during charrettes, students attending their classes will either sleep or sit as if in a state of semiconsciousness, eyes open, breathing slowed, swaying subtly in their chairs, hearing and absorbing practically nothing. Occasionally, after extensive sleep deprivation, students may get a second wind that keeps them momentarily alert, but this is unusual.

Students also learn to capitalize on scheduling conflicts between courses. A favorite ploy is to explain to your studio critic that you are behind in design, normally evidenced by a lack of drawings, because you had to study for a structures exam or write a history paper. In turn you beg for understanding and compassion for your deficiencies in structures or history because you had to meet a design studio deadline and haven't slept for three days. Most students, when faced with the choice, will give first priority to design, knowing that the final jury review is pending and assuming that they can somehow catch up on assignments or exams in their other courses. Unfortunately, if too much is postponed, they may not catch up until subsequent semesters.

The communal spirit is infectious in architectural school, even with the extreme competition and pressure, and faculty and students seem to find ways to enjoy themselves regularly and share their interests and sense of common purpose. Typical of the events that reinforce this communality are informal weekly get-togethers in schools featuring wine and cheese, beer and pretzels, lectures or group discussions, slide presentations or other such distractions. Field trips and travel expeditions are frequently organized, sometimes to faraway and exotic places during summer, Christmas, or spring vacations. Students and faculty often get together socially in small groups, or by class, and the conversation usually involves a lot of shop as well as small talk.

Some schools have annual "beaux arts balls," another tradition borrowed from Paris. Usually planned by students, they are typically costume and theme parties which emulate great European balls of times past. They are characterized by incredibly inventive, outrageous costumes, loud and raucous music, extravagant decorations, generous supplies of food and drink, and sometimes questionable behavior. Balls are held both in school buildings and off campus. Do not assume, however, that all architectural schools sponsor beaux arts balls. With or without them, there will always be plenty of student-sponsored parties, sometimes after juries are over, to release tensions.

One of the more unfortunate traditions in architectural school is final-year burnout. Perhaps this should be called a behavior pattern rather than a tradition. Actually it can occur before the final year. As the label implies, its symptoms are reduced motivation, loss of interest and morale, lack of zeal and commitment, and an overwhelming desire just to graduate and move on. Some years burnout seems to run rampant, like a plague, whereas in other years it is scarcely detectable.

To fathom this phenomenon, one must first recall the intensity and pace of work in the first one or two years in architectural school, when the learning curve rises steeply and, for most students, morale and educational gratification run high. Regardless of what occurs in subsequent years, it is difficult for any program to sustain the rigor and rate of discovery experienced in the beginning years. Even the trials and tribulations described earlier contribute to the exhilaration and peer-group coherence of the initial year or two. But things change, and later burnout is attributable to several of these changes.

First, attrition and dropping out may affect students in a class, especially when friends or talented colleagues disappear. Second, some of the mystery of architecture and design vanishes, making the process seem somehow less intriguing or challenging than before. Third, work is done with increasing independence on the part of students and decreasing intervention by teachers, and some students miss the boot camp, basic training unity of the beginning year or two. Indeed, some may miss it because they are unable to perform well without it. Fourth, students may begin feeling that architecture isn't their "bag," that it's too competitive or unrewarding. If they are not excelling, they simply may be disappointed in themselves and unwilling to be second best. Finally, they may genuinely lose interest while finding new interests, being distracted by economic or romantic circumstances.

All of these changes can produce the same effect: poorer work, cynicism, boredom, and, in some cases, the abandonment of architecture, either temporarily or permanently. As suggested earlier, the concentration demanded by architectural work makes success elusive when there are competing distractions or obligations. Even talented students take leaves of absence, or postpone taking courses, when circumstances outside of school inhibit their in-school performance.

Thus related to the burnout tradition is the tradition of postponement, temporary dropping out, or deferral of course work, particularly in design. But this is not necessarily a bad tradition. There is no negative stigma associated with taking extra time to finish architectural school, and it is often the advisable thing to do for many students. Many good architects had educations that required a few more semesters than originally anticipated.

For obvious economic reasons many architectural students feel compelled to hold jobs while they go through school. They may work for architects, but some do other kinds of work unrelated or marginally related to architecture. If such work consumes a reasonable amount of time in relation to the student's academic load, employment outside of school poses no problem. For example, students carrying a full academic schedule—fourteen to seventeen credit hours per term—can comfortably work eight to ten hours per week without jeopardizing their schoolwork.

But students who try to work half-time (twenty hours per week) or more while trying to perform successfully as full-time students are unlikely to do well in school. Many attempt it, and few succeed. Again the effort demanded in school, especially by the design studio, will conflict with job demands. And time and energy expended on a job will detract from work in school. In the long run it is better to forgo those extra weekly hours in a job, even at the cost of incurring debt, than to compromise the quality of one's professional education.

The traditions mentioned here are all part of the architectural school experience, but the experience cannot be fully appreciated without some understanding of those who teach architecture. So read on, for it is the professors—and what they profess—that kindle the fires of learning.

5

Professors and What They Profess

Preceding chapters hinted at the importance of architectural school faculty in determining the quality and direction of a program, but they did little to characterize the individual faculty types one might expect to encounter, nor what they profess. Schools of architecture attract a rich and complex variety of individual personalities, most of whom love teaching and the stimulation of an academic environment. But architects are especially iconoclastic and individualistic, and they tend to breed more of the same in each new generation of disciples. Therefore, what follows is an attempt to provide some insight into the nature of teachers of architecture.

The Professors

Scholars

In architectural school, traditional scholars are, for the most part, historians. Their work, outside of teaching classes, is focused on research, the writing of books and articles for scholarly journals, lecturing, and the attending of conferences with other like-minded scholars. Their work might focus on specific periods and places, stylistic movements of the past, or individual architects whose work may or may not be well known. They usually have very good memories for names and dates, especially obscure ones, and both their speaking and writing are amply footnoted.

Designer/Practitioners

These are men and women who practice architecture and teach design studio as well. Their time is usually split between office and school, and their teaching is greatly influenced by their practice. They tend to be pragmatic and idealistic at the same time, concerned with the act of building as well as the art of design. Students think of most design teachers in practice as representing real-world points of view and ideology. Often their work influences the work of their students. But their work may also be viewed with some disdain by designers who are theoreticians.

Designer/Theoreticians

Many of these teachers engage in little or no practice, but never conventional practice. Their claim to fame lies in professing theories of design, both in class and through writings and lectures. Since many designer/theoreticians have specific philosophies and design solutions at hand for the eager student, they readily attract students to their studio courses.

Student Advocates

All schools have faculty who identify or hang out with students, who sympathize and communicate with them as peers. They may be close in age to the students or may share their point of view. Student advocate faculty types may spend a lot of time at the school, and they act as sounding boards for students' grievances. However, their behavior may tend to aggravate or provoke mixed feelings (of disapproval and guilt) in other faculty who don't share their advocacy or rapport with students.

Student Adversaries

The advocate's opposite, the student adversary seems to be frequently critical of, or at odds with, students in the school, both individually and collectively. Students may perceive such faculty as acting distrustfully, disrespectfully, and disinterestedly toward them, as being unsympathetic, excessively demanding, or abrasive. Some such faculty seem to have no sense of humor, making them even more inscrutable. But they may very well be among the most effective teachers and, in their own way, be upholding the students' best interests.

Young (or Old) Turks

There are some faculty members who habitually encourage change, reform, or revolution, continually challenging the status quo. They may disregard rules and conventions for the sake of a cause, making a point of their nonconformity, sometimes subtly, sometimes with great fanfare. Often they are perceived by students as advocates since their causes may be shared. Young Turks are not necessarily radicals or anarchists, tendencies clearly discouraged in the halls of academe. To those who resist change or challenge, they are like tiny stones lodged in one's shoes—they don't prevent walking, but their presence is always felt.

Good Ol' Boys

A catchall category, this small group of faculty usually has seniority and enjoys telling stories of "how it used to be." Some may be burnt out as teachers, having run out of ideas or become bored with repeating the same thing year after year. Others, however, may set much of the tone of the school and influence school policy and management. They may be prone to share gossip, shoptalk, and rounds of drinks. Old boys in a school may symbolize permanence and continuity to some, decadence and atrophy to others. Rarely are there any good ol' girls in this group, but this may change as more women join faculties.

Logicians

Logicians circumvent the uncertainty and subjectivity of architectural design. They have little patience for inconclusive discussions of aesthetics. For them, most phenomena are explainable, subject at all times to rational powers of analysis. They usually adopt the approach of the scientist or engineer while merely tolerating that of the artist. They arm themselves well with data and methodology.

Obfuscators

This refers to teachers whose vocabulary and manners of expression are unintelligible to most students. They are hard to understand and tedious to listen to, notwithstanding the significance or depth of what they have to say. Obfuscators, not satisfied with simple, straightforward language, seek richness and complexity in the use of English and equivalent richness and complexity in the thinking which produced the English. Unfortunately this correlation may not always occur. Related to the obfuscator are the mumbler and the "uhm-uhm-uhm-uhmer." They also have speaking habits that many students find obstructive to listening and learning.

Zealous Administrators

Running every school is a chairman or dean, along with appropriate deputies (titled associate, assistant, or whatever). Many of these are intensely involved in leading and managing the school, and their zeal carries over into all parts of the program. This provides inspiration and incentive to faculty and students. But excessive zeal can prove to be negative if it is seen as interfering, patronizing, or misdirected. From the students' point of view the best administrator is one whose zeal is directed toward advocating and protecting student interests.

Laid-Back Administrators

The mirror image in many ways of the zealous administrator, this type of administrator pursues a laissez-faire policy of management and leadership. He or she assumes that faculty are best left free to stoke their own furnaces, to find their own interests and set their own standards. Laid-back administrators may be active in the life of the school, while nevertheless maintaining low profiles. They often delegate much of the administrative work to assistants, secretaries, committees, and individual faculty members.

Separatists

The separatist is a faculty member who has rejected the "if you can't lick 'em, then join 'em" philosophy and instead embraced the "if you can't lick 'em, then leave 'em" philosophy regarding intrafaculty relationships. Not surprisingly, many architectural schools have faculty who, for various reasons, cannot get along with one or several other faculty. Or there may be a small group or faction that finds itself at odds with other factions. To cope with this condition, separatists may simply avoid those colleagues with whom there is conflict. The source of conflict and tension may be ideological or political, usually related to academic issues. Teachers may disagree about architectural style, methods of instruction, course content, administrative policy, or curricular direction. Being frequently unaccommodating and obstinate in their positions, if not dogmatic and unreasonable, they choose to retreat from the battlefront in order to safeguard their domain of opinion. Some never leave it.

Inscrutables

There are always a few silent types teaching architecture, individuals who appear introverted, reticent, or even shy. These characteristics may be less apparent in the classroom or in the company of close companions. Inscrutable ones are sometimes hard to get to know, both for students and faculty, since they tend to reveal their thoughts and feelings quite sparingly, seldom lowering their guard or exposing themselves emotionally. Inscrutability can be a defense or a wise offense when silence is appropriate or needed.

Shabby Dressers

The shabby dresser is very casually dressed, a bit sloppy, almost as if the look were cultivated. To be truly shabby, a teacher must wear old, mostly unironed clothing ornamented by well-positioned stains. Wearing a tie in fact does not conflict with being shabby if the tie is properly selected and knotted. Even a suit may qualify as shabby, just as certain kinds of blue jeans may be high fashion. Other signs of shabby include partially torn pockets, missing buttons, flys partly unzipped, never-shined shoes, damaged eyeglasses, uneven or undone shaving, and most important, unconventional heads of hair.

Natty Dressers

Obviously the opposite of the shabby type, the natty dresser almost always looks well kept and well groomed, no matter what he or she wears. Colors and materials are coordinated, and styles worn may be either traditional or modish. Everything fits. Do architects' dress habits reflect the way they design or what their buildings look like? Or the way they think? Do clothes really make the man or woman? Hardly! However, in school, a teacher's mode of dress may affect both faculty and student perceptions in some way. Perhaps students are more relaxed with shabby dressers through personal identification; perhaps they hold natty dressers in some kind of special esteem because their appearance "distances" them.

Venerable Heroes

In many schools there is often a faculty member, either permanent or visiting, whose fame and prestige are such that he or she inspires adulation, emulation, and respect. These heroes may be famous because of their work as designers, historians, or theoreticians. They may be seen as great innovators or trend setters, rebels or reformers. Whatever their claim to fame, they tread the halls of academe as special citizens. Students await their every utterance with great anticipation, hoping that it will be of profound significance. No one contradicts or challenges them except with the utmost politeness and diplomacy. They can truly become the idols of architectural education—until they somehow fall out of fashion. Then, if they don't update, they can disappear.

Some -Isms and -Ologies

Listen long enough to any faculty member at any school of architecture, and you will eventually be able to identify what he or she is advocating or professing. I refer here not to the specific subject matter they teach but rather to the more general philosophy, cause, or movement to which they subscribe, no matter what courses they are responsible for.

Any teacher offering instruction in a given subject, say architectural history or design, inevitably brings to the subject his or her own beliefs and values about the world—about culture, religion, social behavior, politics, economics, and aesthetics. For some this set of beliefs may actually be organized into a formalized, personal ideology, or philosophy, which continually influences opinions and actions, including what we convey to others as teachers. Even the teaching of a subject which appears to be value free and nonideological, such as structural analysis, drawing, or physics, may be accompanied by subtle expressions of the teacher's beliefs and philosophy. Course readings, subtopics, and organization imply a network of values advocated by the teacher. Thus teachers can be very powerful; they transmit much more than information and techniques.

Architects and architectural educators develop such philosophies because making good architecture requires more than good engineering. The engineer, after sufficiently defining the problem to be solved (ventilate a space or land a human on the moon, for example), sets about designing a system to solve the stated problem most efficiently. Efficiency is measurable by applying specific evaluation criteria such as least cost, highest yield, least weight, greatest speed or strength, fewest number of parts, or easiest fabrication. Subjective judgment enters into selection and weighting of criteria, since most engineering design requires trade-offs between advantages and disadvantages.

The architect, like the engineer, tries to "optimize" building performance, as if buildings could be solutions to well-defined problems. But architecture, being more than habitable engineered construction, is an ill-defined problem. Buildings do more than provide shelter and space for human activity. Architecture affects our feelings and emotions; it engages our intellect. Since it has always been seen, thought of, and taught as a form of art and aesthetic expression for which appropriate philosophies are needed, such philosophies have been generated and used to justify design decisions (when objective evaluation criteria are absent) or to uncover and explain the meaning of architecture. The fun of philosophizing derives from the huge assortment of available philosophies, none of which can be demonstrated to be the "right" one or the "wrong" one with conclusive proof.

What then are some of the -isms and -ologies professed by architecture school faculty, those beliefs and values which clearly impinge on architectural education and practice? Most of the philosophies that interest us relate to one or more of the following:

Formal composition, morph*ology*

History, histori*cism,* and historic preservation

Science and engineering, techn*ology*

Human behavior, soci*ology* and psych*ology*

The natural environment, ec*ology*

The urban environment, urban*ism*

Symbol*ism,* mysti*cism,* and the*ology*

Pragmat*ism* and functional*ism*

Capital*ism,* social*ism,* fa*cism,* and commun*ism*

Management and method*ology*

Like so many other lists, this list contains generalities and overlaps. However, it provides guideposts for the ensuing discussion of what we professors are continually espousing in the cause of architecture.

Morphology

In biology the study of the form and shape of organisms is called "morphology." An organism is, by definition, a whole and complete thing or biological system, something contained and circumscribed. In architecture, by analogy, we talk of morphology with respect to building form. Unlike natural organisms, architecture is human-made and takes its form, in part, through an act of will of the designer. Although there can be many forces acting on the designer and the design, they may nevertheless be insufficient to generate an inevitable, natural form which all would agree is the "right" form. The willful act then becomes indispensable, and it is at this point that the designer may turn to a philosophy or theory of architectural morphology.

Architectural "morphologists" invent geometries, shapes, and patterns whose purpose is to organize and regulate the spaces, structures, surfaces, and volumes of buildings. These geometries or patterns serve to unify often complex buildings into "organic" wholes, to make parts of buildings seem to belong compositionally to the whole. The sources of the geometry or patterns may be quite arbitrary and abstract, or they may be based on some system of proportion or idealized mathematical relationships not readily perceived. Rhythm and repetition are among the most important characteristics of such systems.

Examples of the morphologist's philosophy in action are in great supply. The plans and facades of villas designed by the sixteenth-century architect Andrea Palladio, which have had great influence on domestic western architecture ever since, exemplify the use of mathematical proportioning to achieve harmony and visual interrelationships between building volume, rooms, and exterior walls. Ratios established between widths, lengths, and heights of elements—rooms, courts, facades, and components of facades (such as columns, pilasters, and pediments)— permeate the entire design. Often architects of the Renaissance,

Corbusier's "Modulor" proportioning system.

and Roman builders before them, developed elaborate systems of proportioning derived from musical harmony ratios in the belief that such ratios were natural, and what was natural for the ear must be natural for the eye.

The use of planning grids in two and three dimensions represents another commonly encountered philosophy of morphological organization. Taken to its extreme in the twentieth-century office building, this method of planning can be found throughout history—in the layout of towns and cities, Roman camps, and ancient mosques. Some grids are not rectangular. Grid networks can be based on triangles, hexagons, octagons, and even circles.

Akin to grid-based design is axis-based design. The underlying philosophy of organization is to create one or more axes about which a composition is centered or arranged, often with observable symmetry and balance of elements found on opposing sides of the axes. Ideally the ends of the axes are marked by appropriate focal elements which visually terminate the axes, elements such as towers, sculptures, gates, or gazebos. Of course, where there is axial symmetry, there can also be axial asymmetry. Thomas Jefferson's design of the campus and rotunda at the University of Virginia illustrates well the use of symmetrical axiality as a philosophy of design. Le Corbusier's design for the government center at Chandigarh illustrates asymmetrical axiality, whereas the buildings themselves illustrate how a morphologist creates compositions in plan and elevation using mixtures of grids and proportioning systems, rhythm and repetition.

The Chandigarh buildings show still another aspect of morphological design philosophy, that of the ideal geometrical solid. Cubes, pyramids, cylinders, spheres, and, less solidly, planes are seen as basic, natural, irreducible building blocks. These "ideal," or Platonic, volumes are universally understood and recognized, are mathematically and precisely describable, and can be combined with one another, or repeated, in an infinite number of ways. Thus, by manipulating these solid forms—cutting parts of them away, perforating them, slicing them open,

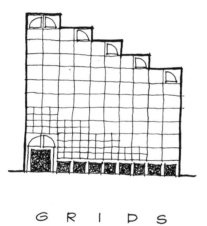

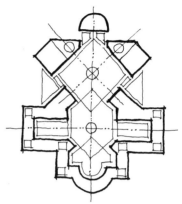

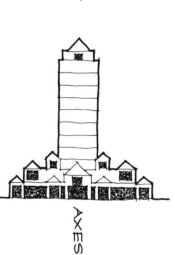

G R I D S

AXES

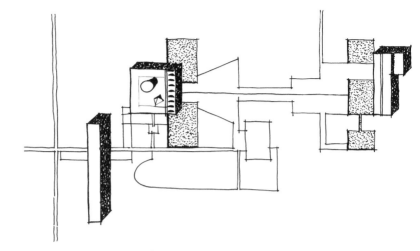

Chandigarh's site plan (from left to right, the Secretariat, the Assembly Building, and the High Court).

fusing them together, stretching or distorting them—the architect can accommodate any human activity and still achieve formal unity, since the architectural composition is predicated on the use of natural, familiar, and idealized geometrical solids. Yet this design philosophy is not inevitable; it cannot be proved "right" or "perfect." It is simply another tactic contributing to the strategy of morphological design.

Historicism

Architectural history has always been a source of design inspiration for architects, students, and teachers. The past teaches us not only what has occurred but also what might occur, or recur, in the future of architecture. But there are different ways to react to history in making architecture. One is to extract conceptual lessons, which transcend specific periods or places, so that the lessons learned may be readily applied when and where appropriate today. For example, a morphologist might admire Palladio's exploitation of juxtaposed, solid volumes and do likewise in a contemporary structure, but without attempting to replicate directly Palladio's work.

Another response is to treat history as the literal, or near-literal, model for contemporary design, to assume that architects of the past have already designed and built suitable and adequate prototypes for today's world, and that all we need do is update the models. Hardly a century has passed during the last twenty without a period of historicism in architecture, when architects looked back admiringly at their predecessors and emulated or reproduced their predecessors' work. Motivated by nostalgia, disillusionment, or genuine adoration for bygone styles, architects periodically turn back the clock.

The philosophy of historicism, like that of the morphologist, is ultimately subjective. It reflects taste. It can be faddish and transitory. It can prove to be inappropriate or misguided, inefficient and costly. But where an act of will is needed, it provides guidance and resolution. Think about the numbers of revivals that have occurred in architecture: Gothic, Greek, Roman, Renaissance. Think of all the assorted places and cultures offering us models: Japan, Spain, Scandinavia, Italy, France, England.

Historicist philosophy says that rather than trying to invent new architectural forms, we should adopt *and* adapt the forms, building traditions, and perhaps even the attitudes of the past. It says that current design may replicate buildings of the past (literal adoption). Or current designs may borrow buildings, or pieces of buildings, from the past and, through distortion or graphic transformation, adapt them for new uses and buildings.

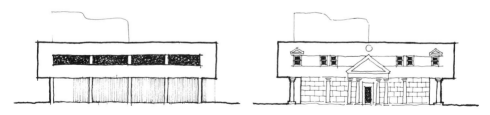

On the left, Corbusier's Villa Savoye exemplifying the modernist, international style; on the right, the villa transformed by use of historicist decorative motifs.

It is worth noting that though architects have perpetually vacillated about the role of history, sometimes repeating it, sometimes adding new things to it, the American public has always been fundamentally historicist in its design taste. American homes, furniture, building decoration, housewares, and textiles are overwhelmingly "traditional" in style, that is to say, historicist. We harbor some sort of tenacious, untutored reverence for a past, much of which was not even ours. So-called "modern" design has never been popular or widely accepted, except for machines (airplanes, autos, computers, stereos). And many machines can be found housed in historicist packages or with historicist ornamentation.

It is not uncommon to find historicists and antihistoricists among architectural school faculty. The former avow the validity and universality of historical precedent, encouraging students to look to the past for design solutions and stylistic motifs transferable to the present. The latter advocate the study of history as a source for concepts, seeking to understand building typologies and styles as products of specific historical pressures incomparable to the pressures of the present. They admire and scrutinize history, but their aim is to search continually for new forms of architectural expression without reproducing forms that, to them, belong to a different age.

Although labels are often misleading and simplistic, perhaps they will help the reader in sorting out these positions. The historicist philosophy may be equated with "post modernism," while "modernism" is equated with antihistoricist philosophy. This reflects the tendency of most twentieth-century "modern" architects to reject the incorporation of historical motifs, styles, or vocabulary (such as Doric columns) in twentieth-century buildings. Their argument (or philosophy) holds that (1) such elements are useless and costly, (2) we don't build today as we did in the past, (3) historicist or revivalist buildings are basically phony, impure, and contrived, (4) such designs are an insult and affront to buildings and architects of the past, and (5) historicism as a design philosophy is a "cop-out," a refusal to confront the demands and creative opportunities of the present and future.

The historicists rebut, sometimes with much greater voice. Their assertions are that like the American household, buildings want to be historically reverential and referential, to remind us of other times and places. Abstract, morphologically motivated design is for them not enough if it ignores the past. Modern buildings are "meaningless," too pure, too simple, too slick, too impersonal, and too practical. They like ornament and decoration, central hallways and symmetry, pediments and double-hung windows. Above all, they argue, historicism responds to a need in people—not just architects—to relate to the past in a direct way.

Not every architect or teacher is either a modernist or post modernist, historicist or antihistoricist. Many shun such camps and labels, recognizing that reality is far more complex, too complex for such limiting philosophies.

Historic Preservation

The movement for historic preservation is very much alive, although it is not really a design philosophy. Preservationists have greatly multiplied in number over the past couple of decades, not surprising in the wake of bulldozers tearing down irreplaceable buildings and pieces of cities in the name of urban renewal. Many people have become sensitized to the desirability of preserving worthy or significant old buildings, if we have a choice to do so. Such structures may indeed possess political, cultural, commercial, or aesthetic significance, and they are undeniably part of our architectural history and heritage.

Preservation of an old historic building may lead to restoration of the building's original use and appearance in toto or to its adaptation for new uses within its preserved exterior shell. Jefferson's Monticello and Mt. Vernon, where George Washington lived, are preserved historic buildings restored to their original condition. San Francisco's Chocolate Factory and Boston's Quincy Market are preserved structures that have been adapted for new, commercial uses. Sometimes older buildings are preserved, either whole or in part (often facade only), and incorporated into new construction that abuts or envelopes them.

Unfortunately architectural preservationism and preservationists can get carried away. They sometimes appear to want to save *any* and *all* buildings that can be classified as old or historic, regardless of their age, historical significance, or aesthetic merit. Perhaps this is a percentage strategy—go for saving everything and hope to save half. On the other hand, it may be unrealistic and undesirable. Many old buildings are not worth saving. They may be unsightly, unsound, uneconomical to maintain, and of no historical import. Architects and the public must therefore exercise some discretion and judgment, either preserving or demolishing on the basis of informed appraisals of a building's historical value, not just because of its age.

Technology

The technologies of building have always fascinated and motivated architects. The engineer in us, aroused by the "workings" of things mechanical and constructed, likes to figure them out. But technology has also been a source of inspiration and aesthetic invention for many architects, not just an end in itself or means to an end. For them technology can generate architectural art as much as any other source of inspiration.

Architects who profess the art and science of technology may not be engineers. Indeed, many approach design intuitively and qualitatively, avoiding computational involvement. Others are drawn to the precision, relative certainty, and potential conclusiveness to which rigorous analysis and calculation can lead. They tend to be skeptical of the former approach with its lack of method. However, the professors of technology generally agree that buildings must be designed with technology playing both roles—artistic form generator and construction technique.

Reviewing building systems briefly, we see that the primary technologies involved include the following:

Materials of construction

Structure—systems, components, assembly

Systems of enclosure—roofs, walls

Thermal control—heating, cooling

Ventilation—natural, mechanical

Solar energy control

Illumination—daylight, electrical

Acoustics

Systems of conveyance—stairs, elevators, escalators, ramps, conveyors

Plumbing systems—distribution of fluids and gases

Electrical distribution systems

Electronic communication systems

Associated with all of these technologies are specific physical components that can be manipulated by designers both to provide the intended technical service and to achieve willfully created artistic effects.

The designer can exploit technology as a means to architecture in many ways. Most obvious is direct expression of selected technical components: the structure, structural connections, ductwork and plumbing, stairways and ramps. This design philosophy exposes and displays the "guts" of buildings as an aesthetic strategy, often using paint in a variety of colors to heighten the observer's awareness of the exhibited components. Also this strategy may even save money if it avoids the expense of concealing and finishing.

Another philosophy that exploits technology is to shape buildings so that their method of construction, their materials, and their systems of environmental control account for their overall form. In other words, instead of forming and packaging a building's exterior independently of its interior construction and systems, the designer can let the building's exterior massing and composition result directly from the ways and means used to construct and organize the interior. A Gothic cathedral and an Indian teepee are both buildings of this kind.

Many modern high-rise office buildings also exemplify this philosophy—continuous vertical tubes comprised of elevators, stairs, ducts, and structural elements (mostly columns) supporting layer after layer of identical floor-ceiling "sandwiches," all enveloped by a "skin," a "curtain" wall literally hung on the outside of the structure.

Technology can occasionally get out of hand. The risk of this architectural approach is that one can easily begin thinking of buildings only as machines, sophisticated human-made objects performing functions defined only by technology. If the technological bias is not offset by other biases, such machines can fail to respond to human needs omitted in the technical specifications and list of performance goals. We sometimes encounter designers or engineers who see buildings only as giant systems, skeletons, networks of ducts and pipes, or beehives of spaces laced by threads of electrical conduits. Most great architecture transcends any singular interpretation of how or why it was created.

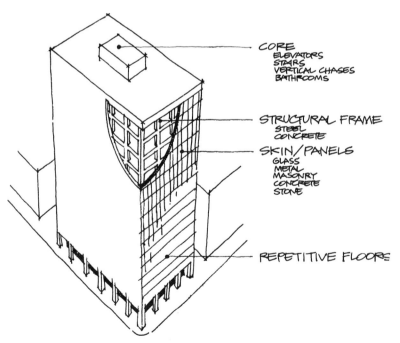

Sociology and Psychology

At most American universities introductory courses in sociology and psychology are available, and many architectural schools advise or require their students to take them. Since the architect must design environments for people, he or she must therefore understand how and why people behave as they do. In the twentieth century our knowledge and exploration of human behavior has so intensified that, not surprisingly, there has arisen a concomitant interest (not quite a movement) in architectural education that advocates design based explicitly on the analysis and interpretation of human behavior and psychological needs.

This architectural philosophy, like others, seems logical and appealing. After all, it is argued, an essential purpose of architecture is to serve people, to accommodate human activity and respond to human needs. When this purpose is met, architecture can become culturally and artistically significant. Those professing it demand that design begin with thorough research directed at understanding in great depth the people who will be directly affected by and use the project under consideration. The architect's client might be a project user, but most users of buildings are not clients in the traditional sense. Yet the architect must know all about them.

User and behavioral research was tailor-made for architectural academe, where research of any kind is both rare and potentially remunerative, no matter how effective. Social science research is especially attractive to many architectural educators because it is frequently conjectural and nonquantitative, just like architectural design. Further, by amassing adequate research-based data and theories about user needs and behavior, the designer can establish seemingly objective design goals and evaluation criteria, despite the subjective judgments that may have crept in.

For example, it is generally agreed that design for special population groups, such as the elderly, the handicapped, the hospitalized, or the imprisoned, requires extensive knowledge of user characteristics. As a result architects today can be far more effective in designing facilities for these groups because they have developed considerable knowledge, through both experience and structured research, about individual and group behavior of such users.

But the reader should note that even without such information, the architect can call on personal experience and observations to predict or anticipate human behavior—an intuitive rather than scientific approach can be remarkably reliable. Many research findings appear to be matters of common sense, confirming what many sensitive architects already were doing or advocating. At the same time the amount of data can become so staggering that the designer has difficulty in sorting things out, particularly when the data lead to conflicting design requirements.

In the design of elderly housing, it's been found that many senior citizens prefer to furnish their own apartments and surround themselves with as much of their personal mementos, furniture, and belongings as they can reasonably fit into the space available. Also elderly residents like to sit and look outside, to watch activity in neighboring spaces or abutting streets. Further the elderly are more sensitive to temperature, tolerating thermal variations, drafts, and humidity much less than younger residents.

To the architect designing a dwelling environment for elderly users, such factors suggest an apartment with lots of wall space for furniture and wall hangings; large windows for looking outside; and minimal glass to reduce heat loss, drafts, and thermal discomfort. No amount of computer time, research, or user interviews can alter the fact that, as always, the architect must finally mediate between these potentially conflicting requirements, making the inevitable value judgments for proportioning and positioning windows.

Sociological and psychological theories also deal with perception and stimulus-response relationships. Sensory phenomena have been studied and can provide a basis on which to make design decisions. For example, whereas some architects rely on personal taste or current fashion trends in the selection of colors, others, believing that specific colors provoke specific kinds of reactions, select accordingly. The effects of noise, or absence of noise, high and low levels of light, and thermal comfort are well known and have influenced the design of work environments such as offices and factories. The need for privacy has been well researched and has influenced the design of the workplace, hospitals, and schools. Nevertheless, the architect must still mediate between conflicting values and objectives, willfully devising an aesthetic strategy. All the sociology and psychology in the world will still not prescribe how, or even whether, to put a window in a wall.

Functionalism

Many architects and teachers of architecture profess what is often termed "functionalism." They are viewed as being pragmatic, usually down to earth in their advocacy, eschewing fantasy and speculation. Their philosophy is to make buildings that "work," that efficiently accommodate the uses intended, are structurally stable, environmentally comfortable, cost-effective, and good-looking.

This philosophy clearly has overlaps with those of morphology, technology, and sociology and psychology since it tends to be holistic and comprehensive. Pure functionalism usually does not consciously begin with the willful act of producing form for form's sake. Rather, the functionalists generally claim that *if* the architect succeeds at making a building that *works*, then it will be beautiful and artful automatically, inevitably, without overtly striving for artistic effect.

Functionalism places great emphasis on the client's program and other project constraints as the determinants of architectural form. Accordingly site and climatic conditions, circulation and space requirements, building codes, construction methods, and budget limitations are stressed as decision-making criteria, among others. Design proposals are evaluated pragmatically. Style is assumed to be derivative, that is, the resultant of a series of rational decisions about massing, spatial organization, structure, materials, fenestration, and proportioning. To many, functionalism is synonymous with modernism.

For the architectural student, functionalism may be one of the easiest philosophies to understand and apply in the studio. It appears to be sensible and straightforward, an extension of the kinds of thinking and problem-solving experienced earlier in primary and secondary school, and in life in general. It doesn't rely on terribly abstract or intellectually arcane theories of design. It is transferable readily from project to project as a design strategy. It could be applied to the design of a toll booth as well as to that of a museum. It's always contemporary, since it doesn't preclude the architect's willful application of up-to-date stylistic embellishments, as long as they seem to fit.

The risk of pure functionalism is that it can ignore real but intangible dimensions in architecture. There are psychic, emotional, intellectual, and visual experiences that are difficult to quantify, specify in a program, and evaluate. They may be consciously provided by the designer, but sometimes they appear by accident or as afterthought. Whatever their source, these architectural qualities are often the ones that make buildings more than just buildings that work. Ironically, many inspired architects, although not perceived to be of the functionalist school, indeed practice functionalism, but always in combination with some other aesthetic philosophy.

Methodology

Perhaps related to functionalism is the professing of methodology as an end in itself. Focusing on how one produces rather than on what one produces, methodological architects and teachers are interested in processes and their management per se. Methodology holds a certain fascination for them, more so than aesthetic speculation. Methodologies can relate to design techniques, graphic techniques, administration, project management, finance, and business development.

The methodologists' tools include computers, flow diagrams, work schedules and charts, analog models, and data surveys.

They study decision theory, modeling and computer simulation, logic, cost accounting, marketing, and personnel management, among others. By understanding and mastering the process by which things are produced, they argue, the quality of the product will be automatically enhanced. Moreover efficiency and cost savings will be achieved. Improved methods equal improved products.

Allied with other compatible philosophies and will power, methodology can help in coping with architecture's uncertainties and complexities. But, like any of the -isms and -ologies already cited, excessive preoccupation with the "how" at the expense of the "why" can lead to limited and distorted results. For no matter how rational our approach in architecture, we can never eliminate the fundamental need for sensitive judgments based on human values and personal convictions which vary with time, place, culture, and circumstances.

Ecology

We are part of the natural environment, yet we often think of ourselves as somehow separate from nature. Oft-heard phrases describe our perceived relationship to the natural environment: humankind against nature, against the sea, conquering nature, struggling against the elements or against nature . . . don't "fool with mother nature." Buildings are "shelters" whose purpose is to separate us from nature, allowing us to survive inclemency. It is not surprising therefore that architects are concerned with how their designs relate to the natural setting, and some have taken nature itself as the generator of building form.

The ecology in which a building exists is comprised of a number of ecosystems. The atmosphere above the earth's surface contains gases, water vapor, and particles. The hydrosphere is the network of oceans, seas, lakes, and rivers, both above and below the earth's surface, made up of water. The lithosphere is the earth's crust, the soils, minerals, and rock formations at and below the surface. Pervading all of these is the biosphere, the animal and plant life native to each region of the earth. Climate, that combination of wind, precipitation, temperature, humidity, and atmospheric pressure, is the natural result of the interaction of the sun with the earth's ecosystems.

The elements of nature, however, do not tell how to design architecture until humans intervene. That intervention traditionally manifests itself somewhere between two extremes. At one extreme is the building integrated with nature, married to the landscape through analogy and avoidance of contrast. This kind of building uses materials of the earth and makes forms that approximate the character of the site. Exemplifying this are hill towns, cliff and underground dwellings found in Asia and Africa. They become almost indistinguishable from the earth and environment in which they sit. Some of the regional architecture of the American southwest illustrates this organic approach as well.

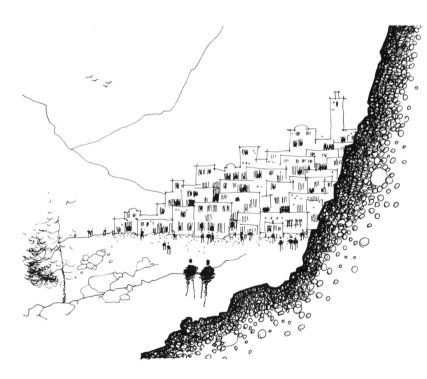

A typical Mediterranean hill town.

Architects inclined toward nature profess not only respect for ecology but also physical design which takes formal cues from the specific ecology at hand. Such designs are thus shaped by the landscape and the climate. Indigenous materials, native to the site, are used. The architecture must be in harmony with the site, unobtrusive and minimally destructive of the land and life forms found there. Highest priority is given to saving trees, minimizing excavation or filling of land, avoiding interference with the natural flow of water, and employing the sun and wind directly to temper the humanly created environment.

At the other extreme are buildings that stand in sharp contrast to the natural setting, in no way emulating or blending with the environment. Architecture and site coexist through a special equilibrium, each asserting itself against the other without yielding unreasonably. There is no attempt to camouflage. Such buildings seem to represent a balance achieved between forces of nature and forces of intellect. The Indian tepee, primitive though it be, is such a building. So are the Taj Mahal, the Empire State Building, and Dulles Airport.

Urbanism

The foregoing philosophy seems well suited to creating nonurban architecture in pastoral or dramatic countryside settings. In cities and suburbs other forces come into play that may render this philosophy, taken alone, inadequate to the task of design. Urbanism, advocated by many architects, some of whom may be urban planners, holds that cities and urban spaces are the ultimate achievement of humankind's building. Good buildings are fine, but they must contribute to making good cities.

What is a good city? you might ask. Most proponents of urbanism would tell you that good cities are centers of *life*—commerce and trade, habitation, cultural activity, education, recreation, and production. A good urban environment facilitates and encourages the movement and interaction of people through and within networks of transportation and open space. The ideal city would have areas of high density and intense activity, other areas of lower density, and areas dedicated to parks and open space. People would be able to choose from a variety of dwelling types exhibiting a wide range of size, style, location, and cost. Urbanism advocates "mixed-use" development combining residential, commercial, cultural, and recreational uses, rather than segregating these uses into separate zones or areas of cities.

Most prourban architects like European cities better than American cities because the former embody physical characteristics that are undeniably picturesque and seductive. These include intensely used plazas or piazzas; spacious boulevards contrasting with intimate, narrow streets and passageways; venerable old buildings (churches, villas, museums, and so on) which act as landmarks and visual "anchors" in the urban fabric; well-proportioned courtyards within buildings; intense sidewalk activity, including eating and drinking; rhythmic arcades or collonades lining streets and plazas; and frequently a common palette of building materials which give both unity and variety to what otherwise might be a visually chaotic collection of individual structures. They like places where the pedestrian dominates the automobile. They like the mixture of shops, apartments, and exterior spaces typical of most European towns and cities, and often found in older American towns.

By contrast, urbanism eschews much of suburbia: shopping centers, commercial strip highways, parking lots, excessively wide streets, conventional subdivisions, and traditional single-use zoning. There is substantial romanticism and nostalgia in this brand of urbanism, celebrating even those urban phenomena—congestion, noise, dirt, crime, poverty, hostility and defensiveness—that so many people seek to avoid or eliminate. Although there will always be debate among architects over what constitutes an ideal urban environment, the prevailing models are virtually all drawn from the past. Urbanism and historicism often go together.

Symbology

Let us now examine those philosophies that teach that architecture can or should be a medium for the transmission of messages. Architecture can be like literature or poetry, communicating ideas or information which the designer/author wishes to express through building. According to such philosophies, this may be the highest plateau of achievement and meaning in architecture, the plateau of symbology. Architecture must stand for something. It is not sufficient only to provide shelter, facilitate work, produce a return on investment, or look good. Architecture must transmit something meaningful to the senses and minds of those who interact with it, who "read" it.

There is no limit to the kinds of things that can be symbolized. For example, buildings can be designed to be mystical, to represent concepts that are theological in nature. Gothic cathedrals are a splendid example of this. Architecture can be rhetoric, preaching specific beliefs or causes through particular use of styles, ornamentation, and forms. For example, Roman classicism was seen by both facists and communists in Europe in the 1930s as the style of architecture best suited to express to people the fundamental dignity, nobility, and correctness of each respective political philosophy, while the very same style in capitalistic America was seen to be especially appropriate for banks.

Metaphoric architecture abounds. Buildings can represent or stand for other buildings in other places (one could make a building be like the Parthenon because Greek democracy was so idealized and pure). They can symbolize nature, or people and their activities, struggles and victories. The Washington monument and Eiffel Tower are well-known symbolic structures, the former symbolizing a man, the latter demonstrating the achievements of engineering and the pride of Paris. Saarinen's air terminal buildings at Kennedy and Dulles Airports symbolize flight and, like the Eiffel Tower, demonstrate the state of the art of engineering.

Buildings can generate responses in observers through symbolic association. They can make us feel secure by being like "wombs"—intimate, cozy, human-scaled, soft to the touch. They can make us feel humble by being like "giants"—huge, heavy, hard, overpowering. Buildings can be endowed with wit and humor, as in many of the Best Company showrooms de-

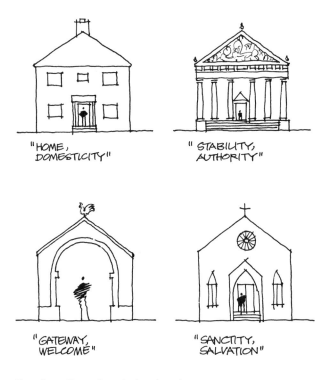

"HOME, DOMESTICITY"

"STABILITY, AUTHORITY"

"GATEWAY, WELCOME"

"SANCTITY, SALVATION"

Transformations of symbol and scale.

signed in recent years. The most common occurrence of message delivery through association is the use of historical allusions and references in buildings. Such architecture says: "I am unquestionably a new, twentieth-century building, but since you perhaps dislike modern architecture, I am going to offer you architectural motifs and elements from the past to which you can better relate . . . an Ionic column here, egg and dart molding there, multipaned double-hung windows . . ." Like historicism this approach reveres traditions from the past but uses them symbolically rather than literally, avoiding authentic reproduction.

In its own way much of the architecture produced by the modern movement in the twentieth century was symbolic, even though many have thought it to be devoid of meaning or symbolism. After World War I architects in Europe, and later in the United States, believed that new styles of architecture had to be devised that would express the spirit and values of what they perceived to be a new age. This new age was heralded by the arrival of new social and political orders (primarily socialism and democracy), new technologies and machines, and new economics. For these architects this meant new building functions and types never before encountered and building on a much greater, mass-production scale. It seemed only natural to symbolize the aspirations of the new age through architectural expression.

To achieve this, modern architecture abandoned traditional motifs to look for a new symbolic language. The new age implied efficiency, standardization, and repetition. It was to be a machine age but also an age of unprecedented individual freedom. So some buildings began to "look" efficient—less ornate, plainer in detail, simpler in form. Some became more "systematized" or machinelike in their appearance. Still others, exploiting new materials and construction methods, became exuberant and complex in form, symbolizing the freedom of expression presumably encouraged in the new age. Historical styles seemed no longer relevant. The new symbology was partly predicated on the theory that buildings should in fact look like what they are or do, expressing on the outside the function of the inside and their mode of construction.

Of course modernism, though no longer a rebellious movement, is still with us. There are still many professing its rightness and appropriateness as the only legitimate symbolic way to go. Their argument is based on universality, since a building that symbolizes its true function can be presumably "read" by anybody anywhere. They design churches that say "church," houses that say "home," office buildings that say "office building," or factories that say "factory." They reject the contemporary use of an Ionic column because, to them, it cartoons a past form whose shape derived from technical, social, cultural, and aesthetic forces no longer in existence.

You, the reader, must now judge and amalgamate these abbreviated observations about architectural professors. If still moved by the prospects of becoming an architect, the next chapter will further guide you to choosing your professors.

6

Architectural Schools— Choosing and Being Chosen

It is one thing to present general descriptions of architectural programs and professors and quite another to suggest how to go about choosing a specific school. Further, what should one do to prepare for architectural school, and for getting admitted?

Preparing for Architectural School

No matter what kind of program in architecture seems appealing, most will demand similar combinations of skills and talents in prospective students: aptitude in drawing and graphics; creative talent evidenced by work in art, photography, or design; technical aptitude in basic mathematics (algebra, trigonometry, geometry, introductory calculus) and basic science, particularly physics; verbal aptitude as evidenced through reading, writing, and oral expression; and some amount of cultural knowledge and awareness. Prior to entering architectural school, it is advisable to have studied basic mathematics and physics either in high school or college.

Be it through course work or extracurricular initiative, any experience creating two- or three-dimensional art is beneficial to the prospective architect. Contrary to popular assumptions, *mechanical drawing or drafting of high school or vocational school variety is not the most valuable kind of graphic experience prior to studying architecture.* Indeed, these can be hindrances if they lead to "mechanical" thinking. This results from the emphasis in such courses on the techniques of drafting, rather than on the substance of design research, composition, and invention.

The development of freehand drawing and sketch techniques is far more valuable at the outset of architectural school. Courses or exercises that focus on spatial perception, manipulation, and representation are recommended over drafting or mechanical drawing. Work in traditional art—painting, drawing, sculpture—will contribute to the mastery of architectural design and drawing skills. Experience in the visual arts, whether representational or abstract, creative or applied, will lead to visual thinking essential to being an architect.

Visual thinking and sensitivity may also be enhanced through seeing and reading about architecture. Those who have taken the time to travel and look at buildings and cities, and to think about them, will be a step ahead. You don't necessarily have to travel far, since you interact with architecture every day, no matter where you are. There are also many introductory books about architecture, and new ones appear with regularity. Architecture is occasionally a topic for articles in newspapers and magazines.

Because architecture is so integral a part of civilization, and because it is concerned with the full spectrum of human activities and needs, it is appropriate to pursue studies in the humanities in preparation for architectural education. History and philosophy of western civilization are particularly relevant. Courses in literature, English composition, and foreign languages hone skills of analysis and expression which are of great value to the architect. Even the study of music is appropriate; Renaissance architects believed that music was the single "mathematical art" whose rules of harmony and consonance formed the basis for architectural composition.

In addition to the humanities, introductory courses or readings in the social sciences—economics, sociology, psychology, or anthropology—are pertinent to the education of an architect. All of these excursions through the fields of humanities and social sciences can continue during architectural school, but time will be limited. So it is wise to pursue them before embarking on three or four years of intense architectural concentration.

Perhaps the most stimulating thing to do before jumping into architectural school is to visit an architect's office and talk with architects in practice. Here you will see the physical environment in which architects work, what they do from hour to hour, how they do their work, and what they produce. You will hear what they are concerned about, what's good and what's bad. Many will freely offer you advice about the profession, about schools, about other firms, and even about other careers.

Choosing Schools

Many factors must be considered in choosing which architectural schools to apply to and then, if admitted, which one to attend. Once again, in an attempt to be systematic, I will try to make a simple list of the most pertinent criteria, although not necessarily in order of importance.

Location

Where is it? City, suburb, country? A school's location is vital to its health, for it determines part of its fundamental ambience and relationship to the larger world. Schools in cities have access to cultural activities and become urban cultural resources themselves. City schools have urban design laboratories at their doorsteps. They can become intimately involved in the urban design issues of the city they belong to, influencing policy and helping solve real city problems. They can readily draw on the resources of the city, inviting people from the city into the school to teach, lecture, or evaluate work. Schools such as the University of California at Berkeley, the University of Utah in Salt Lake City, Rice University in Houston, Washington University in St. Louis, Harvard and MIT in Cambridge, Yale in New Haven, the University of Pennsylvania in Philadelphia, or Columbia University in New York City are city-based schools with strong urban ties.

But other schools reside in more idyllic settings, on campuses located away from cities, in so-called "college towns." Examples of this kind of school include Princeton, the University of Virginia in Charlottesville, Cornell in Ithaca, and the University of Michigan in Ann Arbor. However, being located away from major cities does not mean deprivation. Students in suburban or exurban schools consider urban design problems with equal vigor, but they have farther to go to tap urban resources. The greatest difference between schools located in or out of cities has to do with the quality of extracurricular life. In New York, San Francisco, or Chicago there are simply more movies, theaters, restaurants, museums, clubs, shops, bookstores, libraries, schools—the amenities of urban life—than elsewhere.

Program Type

Is the type of program, as outlined earlier, suitable? Do you want to study architecture at the undergraduate or graduate level? Do you want a five-year degree? These questions may be easy to answer, since they depend on educational background and other factors not related directly to program type. However, keep in mind, as a practical consideration, that more and more

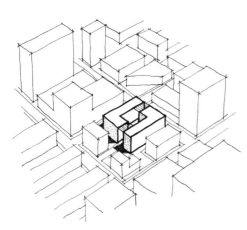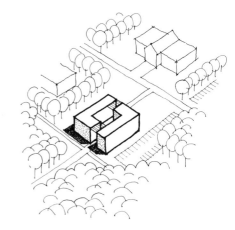

A very urban school, a very suburban school.

graduate architects are receiving masters degrees as their *first* professional degree. This may be of some potential advantage in initially finding jobs and getting higher pay (especially in government employment) over peers holding B.Arch. degrees.

Reputation

Let us not pretend that a school's reputation is unimportant. Schools do have reputations, and such reputations influence who attends and, to some extent, what becomes of them as graduates. Of course there are different kinds of reputations to be had. Some are academic in nature—people think of universities such as Harvard, Yale, Princeton, Cal Tech, and Columbia as academically first rate, meaning top students and faculty, high admission and grading standards, fat endowments, and distinguished alumni. But many universities have departments or programs whose individual reputations may exceed the reputation of the university as a whole. This is often the case in large state universities where specific disciplines have thrived and been enthusiastically supported. Other reputations are related to "quality of life" characteristics—small, big, personal, impersonal, socially oriented (parties, fraternities), or pastoral—which are usually independent of their strictly academic reputations within respective fields. For example, the University of Colorado has a reputation as a party school, but it has many outstanding academic departments.

The difficulty in choosing a school based on its reputation is that its reputation may not be deserved. Or it may not apply to its architectural school. Architectural schools experience turnover in faculty, frequently tinker with their courses and curricula, and periodically modify their goals and directions. This occurs much less often in other professional disciplines. Therefore the prospective student must be certain that both the university *and* the architectural school within have reputations that reflect current conditions, to the extent that reputation is a factor in selection which, as stated earlier, it will probably be.

No matter what current conditions are at schools like Yale, Princeton, Berkeley, or Harvard, one will be forever a graduate of that institution, a member of an implicit network of alumni. Even a graduate who is mediocrity personified may still survive or prevail because he or she is plugged into such networks and because there are people to whom origins matter. Nevertheless, if you are testing for substance, you must dig deeper than networks and reputation. You must get first-hand, up-to-date information.

Resources

Does the school have that combination of tangibles—money for faculty and operations, usable space, libraries, and equipment—necessary to run an acceptable program in architecture? This is one of the questions that the NAAB poses when it accredits architectural schools, and students should do likewise. The only way to delve into this is to inquire directly of the school. Read its catalog and talk to its dean, chairman, admissions director, faculty, and students. What is the student-teacher ratio, particularly in the studio courses (each design studio teacher should have no more than fifteen to eighteen students; less than twelve would be a luxury and more than eighteen would be excessive, unless there are graduate teaching assistants)?

Is there sufficient staff (secretaries, librarians, curators, and assistants) to support the program and keep the place operating smoothly day to day? Lack of staff can seriously impair the effectiveness and administration of a program in architecture. Look at the architecture library. Does it seem ample in size and readily accessible? Ask the students. Check out the slide collection and the availability of audiovisual equipment. These are essential to any architectural program of quality.

Look at the physical environment where you will be spending tremendous amounts of time. Is there sufficient space for design tables, model making, exhibition and group reviews? In addition to studios there should be spaces dedicated to conducting seminars and small- to medium-sized lecture courses, an auditorium for lectures and film or slide presentations. Is there some kind of public exhibition gallery associated with the school? Are there conference rooms and adequate offices for the faculty and staff?

Is there a shop equipped for making models, mock-ups, furniture, or cabinetry, either in wood or metal? How about a materials testing lab for experimenting with structural elements or models? A photographic darkroom and photo studio and facilities for reproducing drawings (ozalid printing)? And plenty of storage for the work of students.

Only a visit to the school will yield the answers to these questions concerning resources and reputation. Facilities will vary in quality from school to school, but all of them should exist or be accessible in some form. Many architectural schools have their own, separate buildings on campus, whereas others are embedded in more impersonal university mega-buildings or building fragments left over from earlier times. The latter are sometimes the softest kind of environment to work in; aging buildings do not imply program senility.

Cost

Today the cost of education has reached such levels that almost no one can disregard it as a school selection factor. There is a point of diminishing returns in expending tuition fees for quality in education. In other words, spending twice as much does not increase educational or career payback twofold. Therefore every student and family must carefully weigh the benefits of educational expense against other alternatives, including forgoing higher education. Until very recently, for example, it was possible to become an architect in most states without ever going to college or architectural school.

There is little choice today about attending architectural school if you want to be an architect, but there is a choice as to cost. The primary choice is between public and private education. Our system of publicly supported state universities has grown in both size and quality during the past several decades. Because state universities enjoy the support and relative stability of continuing, legislated budgets, they have been able to weather the cyclical pressures of economic recession and inflation. In turn they have not experienced threatening drops in enrollments and tuition revenue on which most private universities depend. Further they have not had to increase their tuition fees at the same rate as private institutions.

Therefore students must simply compare the tuition and living costs of those schools they are considering. They must also take into account the availability of student financial aid and loans. Many universities offer substantial scholarships, fellowships, and teaching or research assistantships (for graduate students) that can significantly mitigate the tuition costs. But each university differs in its student aid strategy, and these should be closely scrutinized, along with the competition.

Students

Who goes to the school you are considering? What kind of students are they, and what kind of architects do they become? Never underestimate the impact on program quality attributable to student quality. Naturally, good students are attracted to what they perceive as good schools and programs—they want to be with esteemed mentors and peers. This is one of the great advantages enjoyed by schools with strong reputations, for their reputation alone will automatically attract a certain number of outstanding students and faculty.

However, it is also true that there are outstanding students in every program, students who would excel wherever they might enroll. It then becomes a matter of percentages and ambience. At many state universities there will be inevitably a large percentage of the student body (perhaps as much as 60 percent) that is decidedly of average ability. To a large extent this majority will estabish the academic ambience and generally perceived student intellectual level within the institution and its classrooms.

By contrast, at highly selective ivy league colleges, most of that 60 percent would not be admitted. This does not mean that the programs and faculty at state universities are necessarily inferior. In fact they may be superior, lacking only in reputation. The outstanding student at a state university may well stand out even more. But he or she will find much of the student intellectual climate less stimulating, on the whole, than it would be at many private colleges and top-quality universities. Most architectural schools control admission to and retention within their own programs, applying standards of performance that may be higher than those of the university. And architectural students exhibit a certain esprit de corps, despite intense competition, which one finds in virtually every architectural school.

Faculty

The faculty in architectural schools contribute significantly to the quality of their programs, just like the students. Again you cannot judge the quality of a school's faculty by reading the catalog or listing their collective degrees or universities attended. You must inquire. There are many sources: students already in the program; graduates of the program; practicing architects who know the faculty and program; other teachers in other departments or schools; and the faculty themselves, most of whom are quite willing to tell you how good they are.

But what does one want to know? What do the faculty teach and how do they teach it? Are they dedicated to their work? Do they show concern for their students, for what they are learning? What do they do outside of the classroom or studio—do they practice, conduct research, write, travel, lecture? Have they gained local, regional, or national recognition or reputations individually? Are people stimulated listening to them? Do they demand the best of their students, and do they invest time and energy preparing to teach? Are they in touch with the real as well as the academic world? Above all, are they continuing to grow and learn themselves, to innovate and question, while professing fully and competently the subject matter for which they are responsible?

A number of architectural school faculties have individual members who are considered "names" or "stars." They are usually architects, architectural historians, or theoreticians who have gained national or international reputations for their work or ideas. Teaching is often only one of several activities in which these faculty members engage. Their status as professional celebrities is generally thought to bring comparable status to the institutions where they teach. Indeed, their presence does draw students to the program, since students can easily imagine and anticipate that some of the master's aura and insights will be transferable. For example, the presence of Colin Rowe, well known as a teacher and theoretician in architectural circles, attracted graduate students to Cornell. Likewise Louis Kahn's studio at the University of Pennsylvania attracted and produced hundreds of disciples during the 1950s and 1960s. Regardless of other program characteristics, the presence of a known and respected celebrity on a faculty can be a great asset to a school and its students.

However, there can be a danger in chasing stars. Frequently their time and commitment to teaching and interacting with students are very limited. Extrauniversity obligations may keep them away from the classroom or studio or may compete for their attention even when they are there. They may only teach a small number of students in advanced courses, perhaps only one semester per year, so that relatively few students in a school's population ever participate in featured courses. And occasionally one encounters superstar teachers who are simply less than super as teachers. They may have grown stale, bored, and boring. Or they may be espousing philosophies or ideas that seem no longer relevant or applicable. In any event look closely at who is getting top billing, and get reviews from currently enrolled students and recent graduates.

Prospective architectural students having specific interests related to architecture should seek schools with faculty members who share some of those interests. Therefore try to discover who is interested in the issues you are interested in (energy conservation, historic preservation, solar design, housing, landscape design, interiors, construction, computer-aided design, or history, to name a few of the possible areas of specialization and research). There could be no one sharing your particular interests, and you would certainly want to know this before making a decision.

The array of questions just mentioned will never be fully answered until you are actually in school, but you will get some sense of a faculty's quality by probing a bit. Unfortunately most students rarely know what their faculty is all about before enrolling in an architectural school, and a few don't know even when they finish.

The Admissions Process

You've looked at architectural schools, asked lots of questions, and decided where you would like to study. How do you get admitted? What is the application process like? Each architectural school will have its own unique system for processing applicants and will provide appropriate application forms and guidelines. Nevertheless, there are several things to do and keep in mind when applying to architectural school, independent of particular school requirements. These involve little extra efforts demonstrating clearly the merits of your application.

The Portfolio

Some schools require submission of a portfolio showing examples of creative work—preferably architecural design—done by the applicant. Portfolios typically contain photographs, drawings, and prints or slides depicting the applicant's efforts in design and other areas ranging from the arsty-craftsy to creative writing and mechanical drawing. But it is sometimes the portfolio itself—how it is prepared and assembled, its look and graphic quality—that dominates the admission committee's review. Seldom can an admissions committee predict future performance from an applicant's portfolio content. But if the portfolio looks well presented, if it conveys the sense that the author might really think like an architect or designer, then it may make a very positive impression on the committee, even more than the design achievements illustrated within. Of course, the better the design work, the more positive the impression.

Interviews

Many schools do not require a personal interview for admission. Disregard this nonrequirement. Go there anyway, not only to learn about the place but also to meet at least one or two faculty concerned with admissions. You are, after all, selling and building a case for yourself. Without being pushy, you should try to convey to your interviewer your interest, motivation, background, and qualifications. It doesn't have to be a snow job, but your sincerity and enthusiasm should come through. Be engaging. Establish a dialogue in which you learn about the program, the faculty, and the interviewer (remember, architects like to talk about themselves) while the interviewer is learning about you. A few positive notes jotted down by that interviewer and placed in your application file can have great impact on an admission decision.

Reference Letters

Most schools ask that you request teachers or others who know you and your work to send letters attesting to your skills and qualifications. These letters can be very decisive. And they can be of little impact if they come from personal friends or relatives whose credentials or objectivity are doubtful. To make reference letters count, ask the writers to focus on your academic talents, your educational and professional achievements, your work habits, and your future potential. The best letters are those from former or current employers, and from teachers who knew you personally as a student. Citation of specific accomplishments, skills, and outstanding personal characteristics will be most helpful to admissions committees. Finally, it is always a good idea for the writer to explain briefly his or her relationship to you—where, when, and in what circumstances.

Grades

There is no way around it—grades are very important. Try to apply with the highest grade point average you can muster. However, grades are not everything, and softness in course grades can sometimes be overcome by strengths that appear elsewhere, especially portfolios, letters of reference, and exam scores—or experience. It is not unusual for architectural schools to admit students with less than stellar academic records, but who show great potential through a combination of experience and creative talent exhibited in their portfolios. This is particularly true of applicants who have been away from school for a while.

Exams

These are required by most universities for admission, the Scholastic Aptitude Test (SAT) for undergraduate programs and the Graduate Record Exam (GRE) for graduate programs. Neither exam measures aptitude or skill directly related to architecture, but they do show general academic talent and give indications of how students can be expected to perform. Some preparation for these exams is possible, including preparation in the art of exam taking. If you feel uncertain about your examination prospects, there are ad hoc programs and courses available that aid in augmenting exam performance.

Timing

Since university schedules usually call for classes (and the academic year) to begin in the fall, the admissions process must commence almost a year earlier. Application deadlines occur in spring between February and April, and students are usually notified in April or May. Therefore applicants should visit schools initially in the fall, then prepare their portfolios and application forms prior to the submission deadline. Examination dates should be verified, and exams taken prior to the spring admissions review. Only in special circumstances will schools accept late applications. If you go for an interview, make sure it is before the admissions committee meets to consider your case.

Financial Aid

When you apply, indicate your interest in being considered for financial aid directly on your application and in a cover letter as well. In fact a cover letter is always a good idea, for it can demonstrate your command of language and protocol. The budget process at many schools may result in teaching assistantships for graduate students becoming available for allocation in late spring, so you should request assistantships specifically. Also check into the availability of university scholarships or fellowships which may not be administered by the school of architecture.

Admissions Odds

How many schools should you apply to in the hope of making it into at least one? Well, all things being equal, the more applied to, the higher the probability of being admitted by at least one. However, this has practical limits of cost and time, not to mention appropriateness. I would suggest the "rifle" rather than the "shotgun" approach. Apply only to those schools—perhaps three or four in number—in which you are genuinely interested, and add one more as a backup choice. Your backup should also be a school acceptable to you but not necessarily your first choice.

You may find yourself on a waiting list. Be optimistic, since schools tend to admit more than they can actually enroll, then fall short in their predictions of how many will accept admission after it is offered. This is when they turn to their waiting list. If on a waiting list, there is no harm in writing the school and informing them of your continued interest in attending; help them keep you in mind.

When you cannot attend the school of your choice, you can begin studying architecture at your backup school, complete one or two years in good standing, and then transfer. This entails certain risks or unforeseens. First, without a strong record to support your transfer application, you may still not gain admission. Second, if admitted as a transfer, you may lose some course credits, or even a semester or two, in making the transfer between schools whose programs are not judged to be equivalent in content and quality. Third, to your pleasant surprise perhaps, you may prefer to finish your architectural studies where you started, having lost your desire to transfer to your former school of first choice. This happens often because students settle into a program, become comfortable with familiar territory, and conclude that the backup program was better than they had expected.

Once admitted, you should reply to the school as soon as you have made your final decision. There is usually an admission acceptance deadline, for it is critical to the school's planning to know who intends to enroll in the coming year. If you need an extension while awaiting notice from other schools in which you are interested, write and request the extension. This is also the time to pose any still unanswered questions about financial aid, assistantships, transfer, or advance standing credits. Don't be surprised if some of these issues cannot be resolved until you arrive in the fall.

Feeling positive about yourself because somebody wants you, you must recall that the tough phase of architectural education is only just beginning. The next several years will be exciting, frustrating, mind expanding, enigmatic, fun filled, tedious, exhausting, exhilarating, and outrageous all at the same time. Choosing and being chosen is only one of many milestones on the road to being an architect.

7

After School, What?

The successful completion of architectural school is a significant accomplishment and milestone in the career of any architect. The many years of intense study and demanding work seem, at times, to be unending. Those who graduate are typically only half of those who started. While graduation may signal the end of formal schooling, it is by no means a signal that one's architectural education is complete.

In fact, as challenging as architectural school can be, that which follows may be far more challenging, not only because of continuing work load, competition, and complexity but also because the graduate architect may find a new array of choices and challenges awaiting that were not well understood or even acknowledged before graduation. And every subsequent career path is a continuation of the architect's education, even if it does not entail traditional architectural practice. Therefore it is essential that architectural students look ahead and become aware of their options, remembering that their education will simply shift from the schoolroom to the workplace.

Apprenticeship

The majority of graduate architects, whether possessing a B.Arch. or M.Arch. degree, go from architectural school to architectural office. In many cases young architects will have already acquired office experience working during summer vacations and part-time during the academic year. These first few years of work in architects' offices are the "apprenticeship" years. The term is appropriate, for it clearly implies that the recently graduated architect is still being trained, still learning, still a student.

Apprentice architects, like new arrivals in most professions, are usually overworked and underpaid. They are overworked because they are energetic, eager to produce and acquire new knowledge, and inexpensive to hire relative to more experienced architects. They are underpaid because they are many in number competing for scarce positions, inexperienced technically, and frequently inefficient at performing unfamiliar tasks.

The apprenticeship can be compared in limited ways to the internship served by physicians during their first year after medical school—lots of work and long hours for little pay. It can be justified as a way of getting paid for being a student. In the United States virtually every state requires that architects serve some specified period of apprenticeship before being eligible for licensing as an architect. Unlike medical internships, however, the architectural profession has not been able to organize or systematize effectively an apprenticeship program on a national or regional level, and only a few state architectural groups have made serious efforts to structure such apprenticeships. According to the National Council of Architectural Registration Boards (NCARB) IDP ("Intern-Architect Development Program") newsletter of October 1983, only nine out of fifty-four state registration boards have adopted IDP training requirements for state licensing qualification. They are Arkansas, Florida, Georgia, Louisiana, Maine, Mississippi, Oregon, Tennessee, and Texas.

Architectural apprenticeship employment is very dependent on the economy, with the demand for new graduates fluctuating from year to year. A continuing, systematized apprenticeship program would require steady sources of employment, a unified process of apprentice-firm selection and assignment, and rigorous methods of evaluation. Economic uncertainties, coupled with the propensity of architects for resisting consensus on practically anything, particularly concerning their pocketbooks and their freedom of action, make the apprenticeship nothing more formal than the relationship established between individual architects and individual firms.

An accredited, professional architectural degree, plus three years of practical or apprenticeship experience, are required by most states before examination and licensing. Thus a new graduate architect must first compete for a job in the open marketplace and then hope that the job he or she gets will provide the mix of experience and training needed for independent architectural practice. Many graduate architects change jobs frequently during those initial years, whereas others stick with a single firm, perhaps hoping to become a senior employee or partner. Some work for very small, edge-of-survival firms, others for large, established ones.

In all cases the state where the apprentice architect seeks licensing will demand verification of employment showing that the candidate for licensure has the minimum required practical experience as an apprentice architect. State licensing boards issue standard form questionnaires that are filled out and signed by licensed, supervising architects under whom the applicant worked. These ask the respondent to summarize the type of experience acquired by the applicant during the term of employment, to certify the duration of employment, and to attest to the competence of the applicant. If the total apprenticeship time equals or exceeds the minimum required, then the candidate is allowed to take the licensing examination. Fortunately accumulated apprenticeship time does not have to be all within one firm or one state.

Until recently many states would accept a number of years of practical, office experience—eight to twelve years would be the range—as a qualification for the licensing exam in lieu of an accredited architectural degree. Although most prospective architects must now choose the route of school plus three years apprenticeship, there are nevertheless licensed architects who bypassed academia. NCARB, in a survey conducted in 1980–81, ported that "nearly 87% of all registered architects have a college degree," and "83% of those have a degree in architecture."

There is a tremendous variety of skills and knowledge acquired during apprenticeship, depending on number of jobs held, type and size of firms worked for, type and size of projects designed, and responsibilities assumed. Some architectural apprentices are exposed immediately to a wide range of practical experience, including management experience. This is most common when employed during the apprentice years by relatively small firms (no more than five to ten professionals). On the other hand, most small firms do not have the opportunity to design projects large in scale and complexity.

Graduate architects who work for large firms may gain substantial experience focusing on specialized aspects of large projects but may not have the opportunity to gain the breadth of experience possible in the small office. Concentration and specialization often characterize the role of the apprentice architect in large practices, whereas diversification and generalization characterize many small practices. Likewise large projects take longer to design and build than small projects, so that over a three-year period, one might work on only two or three projects in a large firm but six or eight in a small firm. The apprentice in the large firm might never really grasp the totality of a project and the integrative design process which are more apparent and accessible to the apprentice in the small firm. On the other hand, the young architect in the small office may not acquire the depth of experience achievable in bigger offices, nor have access to the range of expertise, methodologies, and resources to be found in many large, well-established firms.

One other variable related to firms is the willingness of senior architects—associates or principals—to spend time and energy actively teaching the apprentice architects they employ. Such active and conscious teaching involves adequate discussion and explanation of design or technical issues, demonstration, exposure to clients and consultants, and, above all, delegation of responsibility without abandonment or supervisory neglect. For the newly hired apprentice those senior architects are the surrogate mentors and professors left behind in architectural school.

Some licensing candidates approach the examination never having designed and built in steel or concrete or wood. Some have had little on-site construction experience or have never written specifications. Others may have found their apprenticeship years devoid of any substantial client contact or project management responsibilities. This reflects the realities of practice, where firms try to use their personnel to their best advantage, both economically and professionally. If someone is very good at making presentation drawings or models, drawing construction details, or negotiating with contractors, there is a great temptation for the firm to continue assigning such tasks to that person over and over again.

Given all of this, graduate architects should choose employment as thoughtfully as possible, even if jobs are in short supply. The years of apprenticeship are formative. They not only prepare you (or fail to) for licensing and independent practice, but they also establish directions and attitudes that may shape much of your future career and work. If one could choose freely, the ideal apprenticeship experience would probably consist of working for a small- to medium-sized firm doing high-quality design work, being assigned a multiplicity of tasks from conceptual sketching to inspecting construction, and receiving a regular and adequate, if not generous, paycheck.

Licensing

The process of licensing mentioned here is another mini-ordeal on the way to becoming a full-fledged architect. And like graduation from architectural school, it too is seen as a milestone. To become licensed or registered as an architect in the United States and to use the title "architect" legally, the traditional and common track is as follows:

1. Obtain an accredited professional architectural degree (B.Arch. or M.Arch.).

2. Complete a state-required minimum apprenticeship, usually three equivalent calendar years of architectural office experience.

3. Apply for and pass a state-administered architectural registration exam, following which the state issues a certificate of registration or license to practice architecture.

For most applicants, the examination itself represents the ordeal. Why the ordeal, and why bother licensing architects who have already survived the ordeal of architectural school to get their professional diploma?

Architects are licensed because the design and construction of buildings are presumed to affect the "health, safety, and welfare" of the public. Under the federal constitution government is empowered to make laws regulating the actions and practices of individuals or institutions in order to protect the general public. The practice of architecture is no exception. The states want to ensure that anyone claiming to be an "architect" meets certain minimum qualifications for professional competency. Further, in light of the variability in educational standards, states have chosen to administer their own tests for competency. Therefore let's look at both the exam and qualifying for the exam.

Each of the fifty states is no less chauvinistic than any one of the hundred or so architectural schools. Therefore each state has its own version of what it actually considers to be three years of apprenticeship. Some states will grant apprenticeship credit for time spent teaching, doing research, or conducting postprofessional degree studies in advanced graduate programs. Others are stricter, demanding that the three years be composed entirely of architectural design practice in the offices of licensed practicing architects. Only a state-by-state inquiry will reveal the qualification policy of each state.

Over the years the NCARB exam, adopted by most states as the standard licensing exam, has been changed several times in both form and content. This is because the NCARB, in its continuing efforts to improve the quality and reliability of its exam, has experimented with and used successive examination approaches that have been criticized by practitioners, teachers, and licensing candidates for various reasons: too long, too technical, too subjective, too ambiguous, too conceptual, too practical, too irrelevant, and . . . too easy or too hard. As of this writing NCARB has in fact gone back to the older examination strategy consisting of a three- or four-day, multipart exam, comprised of the following:

Division content

A   Pre-design

B   Site design

C   Building design

D   Structural technology—general

E   Structural technology—lateral forces

F   Structural technology—long span

G   Mechanical, plumbing, electrical, and life safety systems

H   Materials and methods of construction

I   Construction documents and services

As the list shows, the current exam is broad in scope and places great emphasis on architectural technology as well as design. Examination candidates who qualify to take the exam usually study for it by enrolling in refresher courses oriented toward the exam or by reviewing their own books, notes, and materials. It is not uncommon for candidates to pass some parts of the exam while failing others, and most states require reexamination for only those parts failed. Some states require that a candidate succeed in passing all parts within some limited number of sittings; otherwise, he or she must retake the entire exam. The NCARB imposes no limit on the number of examination pass attempts. Unfortunately the exam is normally given only once a year, in June, so that candidates who don't pass must wait a full year before the next attempt.

The most commonly failed parts of the licensing exam are the design and structures portions. The former involves the complete design and presentation of a building within a twelve-hour period, and the primary evaluation criteria relate to functional rather than aesthetic achievement. Thus satisfying programmatic, organizational, building code, structural, and environmental requirements is more important than producing a provocative or imaginative design solution. Frequent causes of failure of the design exam are poor time management, resulting in incomplete or poorly drawn presentations, and insufficiently pragmatic design (for instance, omitting needed fire exits or siting buildings without proper drainage).

Those who fail the structures exam are usually overcome by the quantitative, analytical aspects of structural engineering. They falter when faced with the mathematical rigor and dependence on numerous handbooks for design in steel, concrete, wood, and masonry which must be consulted adroitly during the exam in order to answer many of the structures questions. Ironically, this exam is often the last time many architects will have to be so rigorous, relying thereafter on engineering consultants.

In one of its newsletters the Association of Collegiate Schools of Architecture (ACSA) reported the following preliminary 1983 examination results, obtained from the September 1983 issue of NCARB's publication *Certifier*. The latter publication pointed out that the results were "expected to be accurate within a percentage point or two." The tabulation speaks for itself.

Exam division		% pass	% fail
A	Pre-design	66	34
B	Site (written only)	86	14
D	Structure	43	57
E	Lateral forces	68	32
F	Long span	65	35
H	Materials and methods	69	31
I	Construction	61	39

Having passed the exam and become registered, an architect may legally offer architectural services to the public. States require that professionals periodically renew their licenses, but further examination is not required. Most states will also grant registration to architects licensed in other states by reciprocity, whereby a state recognizes the equivalency of other states' licenses. NCARB issues a national certificate to applicants who have been licensed by NCARB examination in a state, and this certificate facilitates licensing in other states that use NCARB standards. For many architects the licensing exam has another significance—it may well be the last examination ever taken.

NCARB learned in its 1980–81 survey of registered architects that after licensing, more than 90 percent were in architectural practice, with about 4 percent involved in teaching. Over half work in architectural firms with fewer than ten employees. By contrast, the 1983 AIA Associate Member Survey, while showing that a majority of the AIA's junior members are pursuing traditional architectural careers, disclosed that nearly 27 percent were not following the "schooling-through-internship-to-registration career path." Thus we can infer that although most licensed architects proceeded directly from school to practice, working primarily in small- to medium-sized firms, many graduate architects travel different routes or take side trips. Let's look at a few of these alternative routes.

Further Graduate Study

Some architectural students, as they near the end of their primary architectural school education, desire further, more advanced schooling. Graduate architects also return to school to pursue new areas of interest after being in practice for several years. There can be dozens of reasons for such postprofessional degree graduate work:

1. To gain new design experience and new insights in a more specialized graduate program—the specialization may be topical

(such as urban design or housing), or it may stem from special teachers and new school environments.

2. To acquire entirely new expertise in architectural subspecialties (such as technology, history, construction management) or in closely related fields (such as landscape architecture, urban planning).

3. To change fields substantially, going from architecture to business, law, engineering, real estate finance, public administration, or even medicine.

Clearly all of these reasons imply a desire to enhance one's knowledge, capabilities, and career potential. In the competitive marketplace where professionals must survive, advanced degrees are seen by many as an asset, and they may be indispensable in some areas. For example, most universities will not appoint or promote faculty who do not hold the highest degree offered in the faculty appointee's field of study. And the federal government recognizes advanced degrees in determining federal employees' salaries and positions. On the other hand, in traditional architectural practice and offices, the holding of advanced degrees may be much less critical to an architect's future—his or her talent and personal characteristics will be much more important. Statistically a small minority of all graduate architects pursue further graduate study after completion of architectural school.

Travel

It would not be exaggerating to suggest that no architect is ever fully educated until he or she has traveled beyond the borders of home territory. In particular, travel to Europe, from which so much of our architectural heritage comes, should not be postponed. And if time and money permit, travel to other more exotic parts of the world—Japan, India, the Middle East, North Africa, Latin America—is equally enlightening and stimulating. In fact American architects should try to see as much of America as possible before settling down too permanently.

The reader should pay particular attention to this last suggestion, for nothing impedes traveling like an excess of obligations at home, wherever that may be. Premature commitments to a job or practice, to a spouse, to children, or to a mortgage can make travel difficult. Vacation schedules, work schedules, financial limitations, and domestic logistics can all get in the way of a summer in Europe or a year abroad.

I stress this because the architectural education travel provides is so vital. No amount of reading of history books or staring at slides and photos can even come close to approximating the experience of seeing architecture—buildings, townscapes and landscapes—in the flesh. This is not just a twentieth-century idea or opportunity. Traditionally architects have always traveled abroad to study the architectural and artistic heritages of other countries, making sketches of both humble and monumental environments. If the opportunity arises, a young architect should live and work abroad, absorbing far more of other cultures than is possible as a tourist.

American architects do have such opportunities. They can seek overseas employment with American or foreign firms, work for government agencies, or join the Peace Corps. They can compete for many travel fellowships available to architects, mostly for European study and travel. Architects who teach can seek Fulbright lectureships and teaching exchange fellowships which permit them to spend considerable time abroad. Regardless of the method by which you travel, it is an experience that forever influences your attitude as both architect and citizen. Time abroad broadens immeasurably.

Teaching

"Those who can, do—those who can't, teach!" So goes George Bernard Shaw's old saying. While this may be partially true in some educational areas, it seems less than appropriate when applied to teaching architecture, where many faculty both "teach" and "do" architecture.

Sienna's campanile and grand plaza (sketch by Stanley Hallet).

Teaching architecture is an attractive career option for those so inclined and qualified. As mentioned before, most institutions require architecture faculty at least to have masters degrees. Most universities allow architecture faculty to consult and engage in private practice outside of school. Faculty who actively practice or consult can significantly augment their teaching income, and conversely, their steady teaching income makes it easier to begin and maintain practices when economic circumstances are unfavorable. Although the salaries earned by teachers of architecture are not excessive or comparable to those in some other professions (see table 7.1), they are surprisingly competitive with the incomes of many architects in full-time practice, particularly those in smaller firms.

Many bright architectural graduates begin their teaching careers soon after completing advanced graduate studies. They may have already gained some teaching experience as graduate

Table 7.1
Faculty salaries by discipline group, 1982–83 averages at seventy-three state universities and land-grant colleges

	Professor	Associate professor	Assistant professor	Instructor	All ranks
Architecture	36,321	28,551	22,887	19,545	29,329
Agriculture	34,743	27,509	23,183	17,277	29,723
Biological science	37,698	28,271	23,679	17,985	31,658
Business and management	41,647	32,844	28,304	20,372	33,841
Computer sciences	41,791	32,288	27,739	21,118	32,834
Education	34,912	27,314	21,828	18,018	27,998
Engineering	40,619	31,534	27,644	19,747	34,827
Health professions	41,913	32,007	26,236	20,686	31,401
Law	50,447	37,157	33,282	23,619	45,123
Mathematics	38,390	28,045	22,269	17,019	30,757
Physical sciences	38,826	28,381	23,130	18,343	33,422
Social sciences	37,498	27,394	21,763	18,729	30,070
All disciplines	38,126	28,550	23,677	18,597	30,631

Source: Office of Institutional Research, Oklahoma State University, reported in an article in the *Chronicle of Higher Education*, July 27, 1983, and reprinted in part by the *ACSA News*.

teaching assistants before finishing school. Initial appointments are at the level of instructor, lecturer, or assistant professor, and they may be part-time or full-time appointments. Schools prefer to hire new, young faculty who show both academic and professional promise through a combination of scholastic achievement and practical experience. Recruiting committees look for good grades, any work independently designed and built, awards, articles written and published, participation in design competitions, conferences or exhibits, outstanding references, and evidence of teaching ability. Some schools won't hire architectural faculty to teach design unless they are licensed. On the other hand, most schools encourage young faculty to become licensed and pursue professional practice, to the extent that it doesn't interfere with their academic obligations.

Teaching offers other significant benefits, not the least of which is the stimulation it provides. Faculty are continually challenged by their students and colleagues. New ideas and information are often first generated in architectural school before finding their way into professional practice. Teaching allows more time and opportunity for research, for theoretical speculation and exploration, and for writing. Good teachers act as exchangers, bringing their research and practice into their teaching and their teaching into their research and practice. And of course teaching is its own reward, offering the satisfaction of seeing students learning, discovering, creating, and growing, in part due to the efforts of their teachers.

The drawbacks to teaching are predictable: inadequate compensation in the absence of supplemental income, especially affecting those with families who are not practicing architects; the demands to be met for tenure, and not getting it; the administrative complexities and breakdowns endemic to universities; the potential for boredom arising from too many repetitions of courses and subject matter, which in turn can bore students; intellectual stagnation arising from insufficient activity outside of the classroom or studio, a commonly encountered condition with teachers who do nothing but teach or who have been teaching the same things for too long. However, most of these drawbacks are adequately offset by the positive benefits cited, or avoided altogether through the efforts of wise colleagues and administrators.

Work in Related Fields

The earlier discussion of graduate studies mentioned studies in related fields. This requires a bit more definition. Throughout this book practicing architecture refers to the specific profession directly responsible for the aesthetic, functional and technical *design* of buildings. Design is the core subject in almost every architectural school, the core topic of almost every architectural magazine. Yet many would-be architects discover, either during or after graduation from architectural school, that *design* and traditional architectural practice are not their cup of tea. They may come to this conclusion because of a perceived lack of talent, lack of interest and motivation, newly discovered interests, desire to make more money or have more power. Whatever the reason, they have several choices that build upon their heavy investment in architectural education.

Landscape architecture and urban planning are among the most closely related fields because they are environmental design professions. Likewise interior design is an allied but distinctly different profession which many architects choose to pursue. All three of these alternative design fields have overlaps with architectural design. Methods and tools are the same. All involve construction. The design products share common territories: cities contain buildings, buildings reside in landscapes, buildings contain interiors, landscapes contain cities. Like architecture each profession has its own educational prerequisites and its own body of theory, readily appreciated and mastered by someone trained in architecture.

Related less closely in methodology and goals are the building development fields—construction contracting, real estate development, and real estate financing. These are not design professions, nor are they constituent parts of architectural practice.

They are businesses other than architecture. But architecture, if seen as a business product, as real estate, is their concern. Construction contractors actually construct buildings, assembling the labor and materials needed, purchasing and coordinating the work. Developers identify markets, generate programs and operational concepts, acquire property, obtain financing, hire architects and engineers for design, construct, and then lease, sell, or use the improved property. Investors, lenders, bankers, and brokers are those who obtain and provide the funds for the purchasing or development of real estate. Some architects are discovering that financing buildings can be more rewarding than designing buildings, if not as much fun.

Perhaps engineering, especially structural and civil, should be mentioned as related fields, although far more engineers leave engineering for architecture than the reverse. It is rare to find licensed, practicing engineers who also hold architectural degrees. Yet some architects could be very good engineers with their mathematical aptitude and analytical approach to design. They may be deterred for psychological reasons, since engineers are often believed to be less creative than architects. Also considerable additional time in school is needed to earn engineering credentials, a major deterrent to the architect. Over time, however, this could change if the earning potential in engineering continues to outpace architecture's.

Finally, we should consider government service and public administration as a special case of related activity. Federal and local governments are responsible for a great amount of real estate, some of which they create, most of which they manage or regulate. This includes all types of facilities, from national parks and military bases to office buildings and housing. Therefore architects have a vital role to play within government at all levels, overseeing this vast network of property.

Sometimes they act as initiators and designers, developing proposals and design concepts. Architects in government may even prepare detailed construction drawings and specifications. More often they act as reviewers, regulators, or project managers, overseeing the design and construction activities performed by outside contractors or consulting architectural firms. Or they may become managers of governmental bureaus, divisions, or departments, concerned with more general policies and procedures rather than specific projects or properties. Occasionally one hears of architects becoming politicians, running for office, and winning elections. They no longer practice architecture, but they may have opportunities to make decisions that have profound impact on architects or on architecture.

Most architects in government miss much of the highs and lows of practice, the joys or sorrows of self-employment and self-expression. But they do enjoy the benefits of stable, steady employment, paid vacations, insurance and health programs, and sometimes important policymaking.

Abandoning Architecture

Lovely as it is, costly as it was, architecture is regrettably abandoned by a noticeable percentage of graduate architects, usually for one or more of the reasons specified earlier. They may also abandon the field out of disillusionment or frustration, reasons cited in chapter 2. They might go back to school and study law or business, sell insurance or lumber, or drop out entirely to spend their time sailing in the South Pacific. In almost all cases the benefits of architecture were seen to be insufficient to justify the burdens.

It would be interesting to compile and compare abandonment statistics for diverse professions. I suspect that architecture would be high on the list, like many nonprofessional liberal arts fields pursued enthusiastically by students only to be abandoned later under marketplace or other pressures. The laws of supply and demand certainly contribute to the abandonment impulse in architecture, with more and more architects competing for less and less work when times are bad. However, I am sure that those who completely leave architecture do so with mixed feelings and a great sense of loss.

Recalling the external impediments and injustices that architects know to be real, inescapable, and beyond control facilitates dealing with and rationalizing such feelings. But the feelings of lost opportunity, unused creativity, and unrealized aspirations must be harder to deal with. The intellectual and emotional payoffs of design invention, the fun of building, the delights of visual composition and form, these are the potential rewards left behind. They are rewards few other careers can provide. At this point the reader should again ask: "Why be an architect?"

III

Being an Architect

8

The Building Process and the Architect's Role

The regulated profession of architecture is relatively new. Yet there have been architects for as long as societies have built, with little distinction between designers and builders. In ancient, traditional cultures and languages, the same word was used for both architect and builder. Construction was an integrated craft in which the master mason or master carpenter knew how to design, to assemble labor and materials, to estimate costs, to manage the construction process, and to erect structures from foundation to roof. Thus the first people to provide shelter for themselves or for others became, in essence, the first architects. Traditionally an architect was anyone with the ability to conceptualize, describe geometry, draw, and construct without subsequent collapse.

But the industrial revolution changed the craft of building. The advent of new materials, new machines, new engineering techniques, and new building requirements made it increasingly difficult for any one person or organization to master completely every facet of building design and construction. Specialization became inevitable. Exotic new structural systems demanded expertise beyond that of a master mason. The proliferation of highly specialized subcontractors redefined the role of the general contractor, whose own labor force built less and less of the building. The complexities of construction became matters for experts who would complement the efforts of the architect.

Architecture became a discipline. The first school of architecture in the United States was established at the Massachusetts Institute of Technology in 1868, and architecture was soon recognized as a learned and governable profession as the various states enacted legislation for the licensing of architects. In the twentieth century the architect's territory has become increasingly circumscribed, limited primarily to the provision of building design services in conjunction with the engineering services provided by structural, mechanical, electrical, and civil engineers.

The conventionally defined role of architects in society appears to be well understood. They are both technologists and artists whose design talents yield buildings with beauty, dignity, drama, utility, and, it is often hoped, cost-effectiveness. Architects' functional and legal responsibility is to prepare drawings and specifications accurately showing what to construct, to assist clients in getting project designs approved by all concerned parties, and to mediate and provide guidance during the construction of projects. As mentioned before, the successful architect must have extensive technical and engineering knowledge, organizational and management ability, sociological and political sensitivity, legal acumen, selling and marketing skills, economic and accounting know-how, social and business connections, and some financial resources, not to mention design talent and a commitment to hard work.

Nevertheless, this all sounds rather generalized, not specialized. If the architect is obliged to be so professionally ambidextrous, why do architects not continue to be traditional master builders? The answer is best given by exploring the process through which buildings are created and identifying all of the participants in that process. Then the architect's role will be clear and comprehensible—at least the role of those architects who choose to practice architecture, the art and science of building design.

How Projects Get Built

Need

"Necessity is the mother of invention" is another old saw that does a damn good job of telling us why virtually all building projects get started. Someone must believe that there is an unmet need, either existing or future. Economists would describe it as identification of a market, or market demand. Sociologists and anthropologists would characterize it as need deriving from more basic human motivations and activities. Some see such needs as problems to be solved, or as opportunities for profit, or as ways to serve humankind. In all cases no project will come to life unless some number of people, perhaps with differing perceptions and goals, agree that there is a genuine need for whatever is to be built.

Once the need is recognized and verified as genuine, then the process of meeting or filling the need can commence in earnest. The accompanying diagram attempts to illustrate graphically this building process, but not from the point of view of the architect. Instead, it shows the process from a position of neutrality, giving no special weight to any particular segment. It is a somewhat simplified, though comprehensive, diagram in that it includes steps that may be inapplicable to certain kinds of projects. It also does not show time and activity durations in a necessarily proportional way, since these vary so widely from project to project. The important dimensions of the diagram are the number and interrelationship of activities.

Site

Along with recognition of project need comes the necessity for a place to meet the need, a site. Few projects can be contemplated without a place to put them. In fact sometimes the site is available before the need to improve it is felt. Whoever undertakes the development of the project—the owner, developer, or entrepreneur client in our model—must eventually have control of a site, either by owning it or leasing it from someone else. With some projects the architect's client may have owned the project

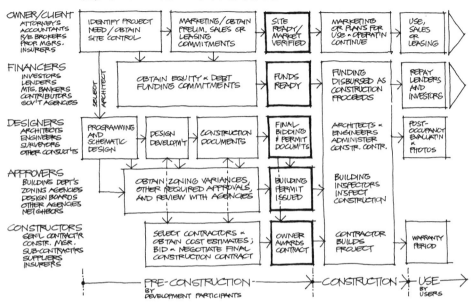

THE DEVELOPMENT PROCESS

site for a long time, but for many others the client may be acquiring the site, be it a small lot, an old building to be remodeled, or a parcel containing hundreds of acres.

With project need and site identified, the owner/client must then assemble the resources and expertise required to transform ideas into reality. The essential resource is of course money to pay for all of the costs incurred in project development—property acquisition costs, architectural and engineering fees, legal fees, project administration costs, market analysis and accounting costs, financing fees and interest on debt, marketing and advertising expenses, insurance premiums, zoning and building permit costs, and, finally, direct construction costs for all of the labor, material, and equipment needed to build. Most of these expenses will be incurred for any project, from building a house to building a new city.

Financing

As the diagram shows, a critical piece of the development puzzle is financing, without which nothing can be built. There are basically two types of financing: equity funding and debt funding. Equity funding represents those monies that the owner/client invests out of pocket, or from the pockets of partners. Equity funds may be donated, appropriated from official budgets, contributed by investors, or raised by selling stock. If a project fails, the equity invested may never be recovered.

Debt funding represents monies that are borrowed by the owner/client with a legal obligation to repay, usually with interest, within some specified period of time. The lender of such funds makes a loan evidenced by some form of note, or IOU, signed by the borrower. There are many sources of debt financing. Institutions that directly make loans for real estate development include commercial banks, savings and loan associations, insurance companies, pension funds, investment trusts, and some credit unions. Loans may also be obtained through mortgage bankers who act as intermediaries between lenders and borrowers. Federal, state, city, and county governments sometimes make loans for special kinds of projects that are deemed to be in the public interest, such as low-income housing or essential, job-creating industrial facilities.

Sometimes the public lends money directly to government agencies by purchasing bonds, which are IOUs issued by the government to finance public improvement projects such as schools, hospitals, or transportation facilities. Ultimately the public is the lender for all construction, private or governmental, because most of the funds that lending institutions make available for real estate loans come from savers' deposits entrusted to such institutions by individuals. If people didn't save, there would be no pool of capital available for debt financing, and very little construction would occur because the majority of monies used for construction and property acquisition is borrowed. Typically no more than 20 to 30 percent of the costs of a project will be paid for with equity funds. Thus the availability and cost of credit in our economic system is inexorably linked to the building process and to the welfare of architects.

Design and Design Approvals

As the owner/client wrestles with the intricacies of raising capital for building, the architects and engineers must develop design strategies for executing the project. As will be seen, this entails many activities in addition to producing design concepts and drawings. The design team must cope with the constraints of zoning regulations and building codes which govern the type of uses and overall building configurations legally permitted on any given urban or suburban site. Designs must be approved by many agencies of government and citizens groups that have jurisdiction over the project, and this may take substantial amounts of time, patience, dialogue, persuasion, and sensitivity. In many cities there can be two or three review boards, in addition to the building permit department, who must approve development proposals prior to construction. Each reviewing authority may have its own, separate design criteria and may require several interim reviews.

Usually, seeking such approvals, along with appropriate design advice, is carried out as a team effort, the team typically consisting of the designers, the client, possibly the client's attorney, and other expert consultants such as traffic engineers or environmental impact analysts. It is not unusual for such efforts to fail in cases where proposed development is controversial; many projects rest quietly unrealized in the file drawers of architectural offices.

Engineers and Other Design Consultants

How do engineers fit into the building process? Recall that structural engineers analyze the structural, load-bearing portions of buildings—the skeleton or frame, along with floors, roofs, and walls—and specify the sizes, dimensions, material types, and details of connection for all such systems or components after the architect generally determines the overall geometry of the building. In similar fashion the mechanical and electrical engineers, normally responsible for analyzing and designing heating, air conditioning, ventilating, plumbing, and electrical distribution systems, cannot undertake their work until the architect has provided a preliminary design that approximates the intended, final architectural product.

Civil engineers, who undertake the design of site grading, roadways, storm water systems, sanitary sewer systems, bridges, water supply systems, and other site utilities or structures, are also dependent on first having an architect's preliminary site plan before they can begin engineering design. Architects in turn must base their initial site planning on topographic surveys provided by licensed land surveyors, who are often employed by civil engineers. In the case of residential and industrial subdivisions, civil engineers, rather than architects, sometimes prepare the preliminary site plans from which the final engineering will proceed.

Other specialized engineering expertise may be needed to supplement normal structural, mechanical, electrical, and civil engineering services. Projects such as theaters, churches, schools, hotels, hospitals, embassies, museums, and, occasionally, houses can pose unique (and interesting) problems of sound control and lighting. There are acoustical engineers and lighting designers who offer architects and clients both analysis and design services. Acoustical consultants are concerned with the control of sound, its transmission, reflection, and absorption. Lighting consultants, who may not be engineers, are concerned with illuminating the environment, using both daylight and electric lighting. They focus on the visual quality of light and the selection and placement of lighting fixtures. It is generally the architect's responsibility to coordinate the disparate efforts of such expert design consultants.

Another consultant often engaged by the architect or client is the landscape architect. Although some landscape architects deal essentially with large-scale land planning (subdivision layout, design of parks, urban master plans, and so on), potentially overlapping with civil engineers and architects, many continue to practice design at the smaller, more horticulturally oriented scale of garden and building site design. The latter concentrate on the specification, layout, installation, and maintenance of plant materials (trees, shrubs, or ground covers). The building architect may call on the landscape consultant to provide a complete landscape plan or only to advise about basic plant material selection. Very few architects are sufficiently knowledgeable about horticulture and local ecology to assume this responsibility, although they may be competent to make basic decisions about plant type and layout.

Finally comes the interior designer or decorator, with whom there is surely the greatest potential overlap from the architect's point of view. Hardly an architect breathes who does not consider himself or herself to be a qualified interior designer. Some architects may be heard referring to interior "desecrators" as being among their worst enemies. It is usually the client, not the architect, who decides to hire an interior designer or decorator. What makes life difficult for all parties is that it can be unclear where architectural design stops and interior design begins. It is also a lopsided struggle, in that architects are confident that they can do interiors and that interior decorators can't do architecture. However, fruitful collaborations have occurred.

In residential and commercial projects interior designers, if employed, help the owner select colors, furniture, carpeting, decorative fabrics, window treatments, lamps, and occasionally artwork. The architect's work may not go beyond shaping spaces to contain, and serve as background for, the interior designer's layers of decor. Like any other consultant group there are both good and bad interior designers, some of whom are also architects. For the sensitive and motivated architect, the best tactic is probably to persuade the client to consider the "interiors" an integral part of the "architecture" so that the client will decide that the best interior design consultant is in fact the architect.

The reader might now be wondering about the legal and financial relationships of expert consultants to architects and

Schinkel's interior design for the foyer of a royal theater in Berlin; every surface is accounted for.

other participants in the building process. Most expert participants operate as independent consultants or contractors, retained either by the architect as subcontractors or by the owner/client. In the first instance consultants hired by the architect are responsible to the architect. Therefore it is generally thought that this relationship gives the architect more control over the actions and decisions of such consultants, since the consultants must look to the architect for payment of their fees, a situation in which the architect clearly has real leverage.

On the other hand, the architect assumes legal and financial responsibility for the work performed by such consultants since, from the client's point of view, it is still the architect who is furnishing the services involved, there being no direct relationship between the client and the consultant. Further the architect, not the client, must pay for the consultant's services, and unless the consultant agrees otherwise, the architect is obligated to compensate the consultant even if the client fails to compensate the architect. Prudent architects usually insist that payment to the consultant be contingent on payment to the architect.

In the second instance, when consultants work directly for the client, the architect may lose some control over what the consultant does but only if such control is voluntarily relinquished. If the architect resists abdicating and can establish a positive working relationship between all parties, then this form of contractural relationship can be advantageous to everyone. The architect is better off because he or she doesn't assume the responsibility, legally or financially, for the work of other experts—work that the architect is usually not qualified to perform—and the consultants' fees are paid directly by the client without going through the architect's accounts. Still, under either arrangement it is usually the architect's job to act as coordinator for all design services.

A small percentage of architectural firms have become combined architectural and engineering (A/E) firms, organizations that offer not only architectural services but also engineering services as well. The relatively few but large A/E firms design a *majority* of all construction built in the United States, partly because of their multidiscipline service approach. Under one organizational umbrella such firms may have architects, landscape architects, planners, interior designers, structural engineers, mechanical and electrical engineers, civil engineers, and construction cost estimators. These groups of in-house experts play their respective roles as if they were independent professional consulting firms sharing a single office space. The only difference between this scenario and the preceding ones is that the experts all work for one firm, which can obviously facilitate coordination and communication. It can also provoke internal disputes and struggles for power. Nevertheless, to clients, it's the equivalent of one-stop shopping for building design services. Some of these firms have reached even farther, offering construction management, market analysis, and real estate project feasibility services along with comprehensive A/E design services. The only thing they don't offer the client is money.

Brokers

Several types of brokers may be involved in development. Brokers are go-betweens who help buyers find sellers or, more usually, sellers find buyers. Mortgage loan brokers help buyers of money—borrowers—find sellers of money—lenders. Real estate brokers help property owners sell property, or they may assist developers in finding and acquiring property for development. Other real estate specialists concentrate on putting together landlords (lessors) and tenants (lessees), and some of them also assist owners of leased property to manage such property.

All brokers and property managers earn fees for their services, usually a percentage of the selling price or rents received. Architects are frequently surprised and chagrined by brokers' fees which can significantly exceed architects' fees in a given project for what appears to be significantly less work, less difficult work, and much less financial risk. This condition reflects the relative market value our economic system places on each service, so be forewarned.

Attorneys

Some projects are legally complex, normally due to financing and zoning complexities. From the client's viewpoint there is an array of legal relationships, each defined by a written or verbal contract, which further complicates the process and makes it possible for attorneys to earn a living. Attorneys are often called on by owner/clients to cope with these legal complexities throughout each step of project development. Some attorneys are very effective, serving as deal makers, whereas others can impede progress, turning into deal breakers. Inevitably, you as an architect will have to cope with somebody's lawyer, if not your own.

Construction Contractors

Of the relationships and contracts mentioned, none is as critical to project realization as those between owner/client and general contractor. First, construction contracts are almost always the single largest category of development expense. Direct construction costs, along with land costs and loan interest, will typically account for over 90 percent of total development expenses, with the balance composed of professional and other fees, real estate taxes, and administrative overhead.

The role of the construction contractor is paramount, not only because his is the most costly contract, but also because the efficacy and quality of construction have great impact on the economic and aesthetic outcome of the project. Architects are very concerned with construction and those who perform it, for the realization of their design and their client's satisfaction depend in part on how well builders build.

Except for very small projects, such as enclosing a screen porch or building a patio, more than one contractor will be required to complete most construction work. Specialization has been taken to its limit in the construction industry. Virtually no general contractor in existence can perform all of the tasks required to build a project, even a modest one. General contractors depend on many subcontractors to perform certain, specific pieces or phases of the construction work. Further they depend on dozens of separate suppliers to furnish hundreds of different materials and equipment items that go into the simplest of projects.

For example, to build a house, the following subcontractors, labor trade specialties, and suppliers to whom a general contractor would turn are required to execute an architect's design. This list assumes that the general contractor would have on staff the carpentry and unskilled labor force.

Subcontractors and suppliers

Site excavation

Site utilities

Masonry

Plumbing

Heating and air conditioning

Lumber and millwork

Doors and windows

Concrete

Glass and glazing

Roofing

Electrical

Lighting fixtures

Drywall and plaster

Painting

Tile work

Flooring

Paving

Landscaping

For more complex structures such as office buildings, schools, or hospitals, additional listees would include the following:

Steel erectors

Steel mills

Curtain walls

Elevators and escalators

Suppliers of miscellaneous specialties

Foundation shoring

Concrete precasters

General contracting is a brokering operation. A contractor takes the architects' and engineers' drawings and specifications, studies and distributes them, and then obtains or estimates the cost of furnishing and installing every component of the project. To this sum of labor and material costs is added the contractor's general overhead and a projected profit.

In some projects the contractor is selected during the early design phases, working closely with the architect and owner/client to monitor probable construction costs, and a final construction contract is negotiated as drawings are completed. This can save time and, potentially, money, since the contractor actually participates in making cost-affecting design decisions. Many times, however, it is in the owner/client's interest to solicit competitive bids from several general contractors. Although this takes more time than the negotiated-contract approach, it can yield the lowest price if contractors are reasonably competitive and anxious to bid seriously. Prudent owners and architects award the contract to the lowest bidder who is financially and technically qualified.

Once a contract is signed, the general contractor orders and purchases the needed materials, executes subcontracts, organizes and coordinates suppliers and subcontractors, and, in effect, sells the project to the owner/client at a marked-up price. Construction is supposed to be carried out in strict accordance with the architect's plans as approved by the owner/client. General contractors, like every subcontractor and supplier, have one primary business motive: to make a profit. Therefore it is their business to buy low and sell high, putting them into periodic conflict with the architect and owner/client, since the latter's objective, among others, is to get the most for the money from the contractor. This explains further why project owners, architects, and contractors are usually separate entities linked together by contractual agreements, with the architect being primarily responsible for protecting the client's interest while simultaneously being fair to the contractor. In fact during construction the architect has an obligation to resolve disputes objectively between owner and contractor, even if it means siding with the contractor.

Role Playing

Remember that different roles in the building process may be played by a single individual or entity. For example, an architect's client can also act as his or her own general contractor. Large developers who build housing or commercial projects may have their own construction contracting department, design department, financing brokerage, real estate brokerage, property management department, or accounting and legal staffs under one corporate roof. Other developers are literally one-person operations, requiring only a telephone, a mailing address, a long list of loyal subcontractors, suppliers, and consultants, and frequently minimal working capital (but lots of borrowing potential).

Similarly architects may step out of their design role by buying property, raising money, constructing or renovating buildings, and then selling or leasing them for a profit (or loss). Again, like the big corporate entrepreneur, the architect can assume the roles of developer and borrower, contractor, marketer, and investor, as well as designer. Nevertheless, each separate role must be played, each demands certain, distinguishable knowledge and actions, and each may draw on widely divergent talents or capabilities in the person assuming the roles. Note also that there are possible conflicts of interest in playing multiple roles, the most apparent arising when architects act as general contractors for their clients. Until recently this was considered unethical by the American Institute of Architects. This is no longer so, the theory being that adequate disclosure of financial interests by the architect to the client somehow eliminates the presumed conflict of interest.

Our diagram shows that project construction cannot begin until all of the proverbial ducks are in a row. Adequate funds must be secured and ready to flow; property control or ownership must be finalized; architectural and engineering design documents must be completed and approved by all authorities; building permits must be issued; construction contracts must be bid for, negotiated, and signed; insurance must be in force; preliminary leasing, sales, or market demand must be verified; and other minor though essential tasks must be finished. Unless all of these preconstruction necessities are checked off, the project cannot proceed. It is not uncommon for the development process to reach the point of construction commencement only to be stopped, sometimes forever, because one of these contingent necessities remains unsatisfied. Ask any architect, and you can again see file drawers with completely drawn projects that went unbuilt because financing fell through, or zoning variances were denied, or title to the property became clouded, or citizen-sponsored lawsuits tied up the developer for years beyond the time when the project had been feasible.

Once begun, the construction period for a project can last for months or years, depending on the size and complexity of the project. House remodelings are notorious for taking as long to complete as new homes or office buildings. Delays are the norm, resulting from labor strikes, material and labor shortages, bad weather, unforeseen soil conditions, errors or changes in design, or poor construction planning. Some projects seem to be under construction forever—hospitals, college campuses, transportation terminals. During construction the architect's role changes from design to clarification and periodic verification of the contractor's work. The architect continues to interact with the property owner, tenants, leasing agents, lenders, and building departments having jurisdiction over the project.

Users

The diagram makes note of the "user." Users may never have a contract with any of the aforementioned participants in the development process, but they are very real clients to the architect.

User's may be thought of as the ultimate consumers of architecture, the people who finally see, touch, occupy, live in, and move through the finished product. Included are neighbors, those who work in buildings, visit them, or shop in them. They are the collective constituency of those involved directly in the building process. Building codes and zoning regulations protect them, not the architect, owner, contractor, or lenders.

It is therefore incumbent on the architect always to be aware of an invisible, nonpaying client sitting at the conference table whose interests must be duly represented and advocated by the architect. If ignored or overlooked, the neglected user can find recourse as if there had been a contract, suing everyone in sight if he or she is injured, complaining ceaselessly, withholding rent if uncomfortable or unsafe, refusing to buy or rent (and thereby leading projects to insolvency), and otherwise holding architects and builders in low esteem, perhaps even publicly. So never forget or shortchange the user. And when possible, try to invite real, in-the-flesh users to the design conference table.

9

How Architects Work

Article one of the AIA standard form agreement between owner/client and architect (AIA Document B141) describes the architect's services and responsibilities, and in the interest of brevity and conciseness, I have taken the liberty of summarizing them here. As you will see, the contract does two things at once. First, it says *what* the architect is going to do. Second, through well-chosen words and ordering of paragraphs, it suggests *how* the architect will perform the services. Theoretically such a description of services should tell us what we want to know about the work architects do. In this the AIA document fails. But it does give us an outline we can fruitfully flesh out.

Basic architectural services consist of five phases, and the architect's work product is indicated for each phase.

Phase	Work product
1. Schematic design—analysis of the owner's program, site, and budget; preliminary design studies in sketch form and a preliminary estimate of probable construction cost.	Program diagrams Function diagrams Site plans, floor plans, sections, elevations, perspectives, models, in sketch form
2. Design development—further development of the schematic design; definition of basic project systems and materials; decision on	More precise plans, sections, elevations, site plan drawings; more realistic perspectives and study models

project size, dimensions, architectural character; update estimate.

3. Construction documents —detailed design of the project, including all engineering design, selection of materials, establishment of dimensions, construction assembly details, appropriate construction notes (required to obtain construction bids and building permits).

Working drawings

Specifications

Bidding information

4. Bidding or negotiation—during or after completion of the construction documents, assisting the client in finding, screening, selecting qualified general contractors from whom bids may be obtained or with whom a contract may be negotiated; assisting the client in reviewing bids and awarding contracts.

Contractor's bids

Construction contracts

Modified design documents to meet budget limits

5. Construction administration—representing or assisting the client in administering the construction contract, including making design changes, site visits, reviewing the contractor's work, requests for payment, selecting colors and previously unspecified items, checking shop drawings prepared by fabricators, mediating disputes between contractor and owner.

Design change documents

Field reports of site visits

Certifications for payment and completion

Beyond these five phases the AIA contract goes on to describe so-called additional services which may be provided if the client wishes and the architect agrees. Otherwise they are normally excluded from basic services. These additional services can include economic feasibility studies, detailed cost estimations, interior design (for furniture and furnishings), surveying and measuring existing structures, special design or engineering consultation not usually required, and a host of other extras, all of which constitute, in the judgment of those signing the agreement, work beyond the scope anticipated for typical architectural design work.

This outline of services is more or less chronological, proceeding from the initial, conceptual studies of design possibilities, the exploration of architectural ideas, to the more exact delineation and explication of what is to be built, and then finally to the execution of the project itself. This, for the most part, is what architects do and in the most general way, how they do it.

But let us probe further. As I stated at the outset, this definition of work scope hardly tells us what happens in an architect's office on an hourly, daily, weekly, or even continuing basis to effectuate services and fulfill the architect's mission. Moreover, how are architectural offices themselves structured and operated?

The easiest way to get at the nature of architectural practice is through the specific job tasks that are common to all architectural organizations, be they small or large, private or governmental, domestic or foreign. Making use of descriptions found in various surveys conducted by the AIA, NCARB, and others, table 9.1 shows the many on-going tasks accomplished in architectural practice. The activity classifications need some additional clarification before you can fully appreciate the significance of this chart.

Table 9.1
Day-to-day tasks in architectural practice

	Type of activities involved				
Primary job functions	Draw	Write	Read	Talk	Compute
Running the office					
Client relations	0	+ +	+	+ + +	0
Marketing and promotion	+	+ +	+ +	+ + +	0
Firm management	0	+ +	+ +	+ + +	+ + +
Designing projects					
Project management	0	+ +	+	+ +	+ +
Programming and research	0	+ +	+ + +	+	+ +
Conceptual design	+ + +	0	+	+	+
Working drawings	+ + +	0	+	+	+ +
Specifications	0	+ + +	+ + +	+	0
Consultant coordination	0	+ +	+ +	+ + +	0
Cost analysis	0	+	+ + +	+ +	+ + +
Executing projects					
Bidding and negotiation	0	+ +	+	+ + +	+ + +
Construction administration (office)	+ +	+ + +	+ +	+ +	+ + +
Construction administration (field)	0	+	0	+ + +	0

Note: 0 = almost none required, + = small amount required, + + = moderate amount required, + + + = great amount required.

Drawing

"Drawing" might at first seem self-explanatory, but there are several different kinds of architectural drawings, of which some are particular to each phase of service. During the schematic phase most of the drawing is "sketchy," quick, diagrammatic, at times impressionistic. Soft pencils, marking pens, charcoal, chalk, or colored pencils are used freely, along with inexpensive rolls of thin yellow or white tracing paper which allows overlays of previous drawings to be made readily. The designer's primary tool at this point is the architectural scale; if one had to choose only three things essential to designing a work of architecture, they would be pencil, paper, and scale. Even when searching for

BEGIN:

RESEARCH & ANALYSIS OF PROJECT SITE, CLIENT, PROGRAM, BUDGET, REGULATIONS, HISTORICAL PRECEDENT

PROGRAM: A SCHOOL

SPACE/ACTIVITY	AREA	SPECIAL REQ'TS
CLASSROOMS	8 @ 900 SF	FLEXIBLE, BRIGHT..........
MUSIC STUDIO	1 @ 900 SF	ACOUSTIC, NEAR ART......
ART STUDIO	1 @ 1200 SF	SKYLIGHT, TACKBOARD....
CAFETERIA	3000 SF	STAGE, VENTILATION......
ADMINISTRATION	1500 SF	NEAR ENTRY, SECURE ...
RESTROOMS	4 @ 400 SF	ALL TILE, WINDOWS ....
STORAGE	1000 SF	DISTRIBUTE AMONG ....
MECHANICAL	1200 SF	FAR FROM MUSIC ....

SCHEMATIC DESIGN

CONCEPTUAL DIAGRAMS:

INCREASE SCALE

SITE CONCEPTS
VOLUMETRIC CONCEPTS
PLAN & SECTION CONCEPTS
IMAGE/FACADE CONCEPTS
FUNCTIONAL LAYOUTS

ALTERNATE A   ALTERNATE B   ALTERNATE C   ALTERNATE D   ALTERNATE E   ALTE

SKETCHES OF BASIC CONCEPTUAL DESIGN:

INCREASE SCALE

SITE PLAN
FLOOR PLANS
SECTIONS
ELEVATIONS
PERSPECTIVES, AXONS

ALTERNATE M

DESIGN DEVELOPMENT

ACCURATE DRAWINGS OF FINAL DESIGN

INCREASE SCALE

SITE PLAN
FLOOR PLANS
SECTIONS
ELEVATIONS
PERSPECTIVES
AXONOMETRICS
TYPICAL WALL SECTIONS
STRUCTURAL/MECH SCHEMA

EAST ELEVATION • 1/8" = 1'-0"

DETAILED DRAFTING

WORKING DRAWINGS

CONC. BLK. BACK-UP
FACE BRICK
MASONRY TIES

INSULATION

STEEL SHELF ANGLE

METAL WINDOW FRAME
INSULATING GLASS

MARBLE SILL

BRICK SILL
CONC. BLK. BACK-UP
INSULATION

CONTINUOUS FLASHING
CANT STRIP
BUILT-UP ROOFING (5 PLY)

RIGID INSULATION
CONC. SLAB

SUPPLY AIR DUCT

FLUORESCENT LT. FIXT.
SUSPENDED CEILING

½" DRYWALL ON
¾" FURRING

concepts and exploring ideas, good designers continually draw their sketches to scale. In similar fashion, simple, quickly made study models of cardboard or clay are used to study formal hypotheses.

Then the architects' drawings become less sketchy and more precise, enlarging in scale, as more drafting equipment is used during the design development phase. In addition to scales, pencils, and paper, designers employ parallel bars or T-squares on drawing boards, triangles, compasses, and varieties of templates for drawing geometric shapes. As lines are drawn straighter, thinner, and more accurately, pencil leads become harder and are sharpened more frequently.

Presentation drawings can be done any time after schematic design. Unlike study sketches and carefully drafted working drawings, presentation drawings are explicitly made to impress a client, to show at reviews and meetings, or for publication. They are a kind of selling documentation and may be rendered versions of the drawings produced during the design development phase of work. Frequently they are ink drawings that may be rendered with color or shading textures. Whether drawn freehand or with instruments, they must be drawn carefully and with graphic sensitivity. Often firms make presentation drawings during subsequent phases, or even after projects are built, if they were not required prior to the construction drawings phase.

Most of the time spent drawing in architects' offices is consumed producing construction documents. While only one or a few architects produce drawings during the conceptual design phases, many architectural draftspersons may need several months to produce all of the working drawings—the detailed design—for building permits and construction. Drafting construction documents is the most labor-intensive, complex, and sometimes tedious phase of the architect's work. Up to 50, 100, or even 150 hours can be required to complete a single sheet of detailed construction drawings. In a full set of drawings there easily can be ten to fifteen sheets for small projects and many dozens of

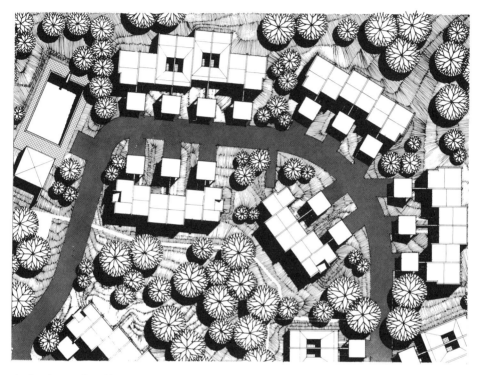

A site plan rendered for presentation.

sheets for large or complex projects, not counting engineering drawings whose number can exceed the number of architectural drawings.

Turning out construction documents also entails extensive coordination within the architect's office. Consider the following which is typical of the content of a set of architectural working drawings, applicable to either large or small projects, and necessary to describe fully the design of a building. Keep in mind that each single sheet of drawing may represent from one to three weeks per person of drafting, dimensioning and note writing. Remember too that over the lifetime of the project, several different architects may be working on the documents but not necessarily at the same time nor with the same expertise.

Drawing type	Content
Site plans	Location of buildings, other improvements, grading, paving, landscaping, utilities.
Floor plans	Location of columns, walls, rooms, windows and doors, equipment, and layout dimensions.
Sections	Profiles of building roof, floors, walls, spaces within, ceilings, structure, and vertical dimensions.
Elevations	Orthogonal views of building exterior showing shape, materials, location of openings, doors and windows, decorative elements, assembly joints, textures and coloration (by notation).
Interior elevations	Like exterior elevations but showing the composition of interior wall surfaces, especially kitchens, bathrooms, and decorated or special spaces.
Reflected ceiling plans	Composition and layout of ceilings, including locations of light fixtures, ventilation registers, panels, sprinkler heads, acoustical grids, and any exposed structure, ducts, or pipe.
Schedules	Charts showing the type, size, and quantity of windows and doors; interior materials and finishes for walls, ceilings, and floors; painting; finish hardware (e.g., locksets and hinges for doors); light fixtures; plumbing fixtures.
Details	Large-scale plans, sections, or elevations of construction assembly conditions (e.g., how a window fits into a wall or a railing attaches to a floor), stairs, cabinetry and millwork, ornamentation, and other architectural components.

All these architectural drawings are complemented by analogous drawings furnished by the engineers showing framing, foundations, mechanical equipment, ductwork, piping, electrical circuits and equipment, along with appropriate engineering details. The architects applying lead to paper must constantly check their own work, as well as that of others, to see that each building component is shown and specified consistently throughout the drawings, that dimensions add up correctly, that no essential item is omitted from the drawings, and that components will actually fit together at the construction site as they appear to in the drawings.

As you may have observed, architect's working drawings are typically covered with notes. These are an integral part of the drawn building design, though in verbal form, explaining and specifying what cannot be shown graphically. They identify and name components and materials or instruct contractors to perform some specific work in accordance with the notation. For example, one note might identify a material as "concrete," whereas another might say that each batch of concrete is to be tested before placement. Often notes like the latter are contained in specifications written and printed separately from the drawings.

The need to write words on drawings has given rise to the architect's art of "lettering," another potentially time-consuming part of day-to-day work. Most laymen quickly recognize the hand printing of an architect, perfected after hours and hours of practice and repetition, drawing lettering guidelines, and struggling to make an ideally shaped "S," "B," "R," or "M." Some architects can letter quickly, whereas others may spend as much time lettering a sheet as drawing it. Press-on letters and lettering machines are available and can improve the graphic quality of a drawing sheet, but they usually require more time than a facile, talented draftsperson/letterer.

Firms have a tendency to optimize productivity by employing people who work fast and effectively in at least one area of activity. Since the greatest percentage of time and labor goes into the production of construction documents, primarily working drawings, firms prefer to hire architects who can draft well and who know how to perform detailed design for construction. One or two conceptual designers can keep scores of people continually busy drafting if there is enough new work coming into the office. Therefore, when a young architect is hired by any but the smallest of architectural firms, it is likely that he or she will be hired to do drafting primarily. Although it is essential to spend some number of your early years doing basic drawing in order to learn the art and craft of design for construction, it is probably not your life's ambition.

Some young architects become "designers," concentrating on schematic design and design development. They may avoid or have little opportunity to produce detailed construction drawings and specifications. A talent for making presentation drawings and beautiful renderings tempts firms to keep such talent doing what it does best. Other architects develop a reputation as "field" types if they prove effective in coping with construction contractors and job site problems, preparing field reports, and following up at the office with memos. If so classified, such architects may rarely sit at a drafting board.

Writing

As you can see, there are a number of functions in practice that entail little or no drawing, for which I have assigned a "0." However, virtually all functions require some time invested in writing, reading, and talking—basic verbal skills that are critical to practicing architecture. To the surprise of many graduate architects entering offices, much time is spent writing.

They must write letters or memoranda to clients, engineers, product manufacturers, and government agencies. Memos and reports must be prepared, sent, and filed constantly. Architects must write specifications, some in the form of notes on drawings, transmitting information about their design intent to others. Architects with management responsibility write proposals, contracts, certifications, and promotional documents.

Mentioned several times earlier, specifications can be the bulk-iest written output of an architectural practice. To beginning ar-chitects a set of construction specifications can appear very intimidating, not only because of its size but also because of the esoteric nature of many of the items called for. However, most sets of specifications are merely rewrites of previously used sets, edited and modified to fit the project at hand.

Much of the jargon and legalese in specifications is probably un-necessary, and certainly much of it is standardized "boiler plate" language that could be incorporated by reference to widely ac-cepted standards of construction practice. In fact many firms now use computer-based specification formats that could be so referenced. Specifications address materials and products to be used, identifying their type, manufacturer, size, and other per-formance characteristics. For example, a "spec" could describe the type of lumber or steel to be used in framing the structure of a building, the type of concrete for foundations, the type of win-dows and brick for exterior walls. Specifications are usually writ-ten and organized in sections that relate to primary building trades and product categories, such as plumbing, metals, car-pentry, concrete, masonry, or sitework.

For each project the architect responsible for writing the specifi-cations must accomplish three missions: first, inapplicable speci-fication items must be deleted from the reference set; second, items left in must be modified, when necessary, to conform to the new design; and third, new specification items, not con-tained in the reference set, must be added if the design calls for them. The greatest dilemma in preparing specifications is know-ing how much to include and how much to leave out, for speci-fying too much or too little can get architects into trouble. Too much can drive costs up needlessly; too little can compromise quality. Only experience writing specifications and administer-ing construction can give you the judgment needed for resolving this eternal dilemma.

When projects are built, most architectural liabilities arise. Therefore architects tend to create and leave written "paper trails" that constitute a history of the project—minutes of meetings, telephone notes, memos confirming verbal agreements and approvals, and letters of transmittal, among others. Thorough documenters are hard to find, since architects would rather draw than write in most cases. So compulsive and reasonably articulate writers are invaluable, especially during construction.

The ideal paper trail exculpates and protects the architect when things go wrong, blaming as much as possible on the contractor's mistakes or the client's bad judgment. Inspection reports, change orders, payment certifications, or general correspondence must always be written with an eye on the potential for litigation if anything done erroneously is admitted by the architect. Obviously it is in the architect's interest to cast favorable light on his or her actions and never to admit negligence. Again, like writing specifications, creating a proper paper trail is a matter of knowing what to include and what to exclude.

Reading

We architects also read a lot. Obviously we must allot time for reading incoming mail, memos, and magazines like everyone else in business. But we must also be thorough researchers, reading research material, reference manuals and handbooks, zoning and building codes, product catalogs and specifications, and contracts meticulously and with total comprehension. Failing to do so can lead to legal, financial, and professional disaster. A few tasks are reading intensive, but the ability to express oneself in writing and orally are the verbal skills most frequently in use, as table 9.1 suggests.

Talking

"Talking" is an activity most of us do willingly. In this context, however, I intend "talking" to mean substantive or persuasive verbal communication, either of ideas or information. Just as we may be astounded by the time demands of writing, we may also fail to anticipate the hours and energy that architects devote to talking with one another, and with their clients, consultants, public agency officials, committees and boards, salespeople and manufacturers' representatives, attorneys, accountants, insurance agents, and bankers. And much of this effort occurs with at least one telephone next to at least one ear. Meetings abound in architectural practice. There are days when an architect feels that architectural practice should be renamed architectural prattle.

Perhaps the most critical talking takes place when architects are selling their services, trying to develop business contacts and secure commissions, and then later when they try to sell their design concepts to skeptical clients or review boards. This kind of talking can be an art form, the art of persuasion and negotiation. The ability to convince others of your credibility, correctness, capability, and even lovability is indispensable. Likewise this art must be practiced when dealing with contractors, many of whom are tough negotiators and think nothing of having soft-spoken, sensitive architects for breakfast. Architects spend lots of time in conversation with construction estimators and project

managers, superintendents, and subcontract trade foremen haggling over bids and prices, the intent and interpretation of drawings and specifications, scheduling, cost extras and overruns, and, above all, the quality and craftmanship of construction work designed by the architect.

Computing

"Compute" refers to the many different types of accounting and computational operations that architects must perform in practice. Some accounting activity in the management of the firm's finances involves keeping track of work completed and worker-hours consumed, invoicing clients and collecting fees, paying salaries and other expenses, and maintaining a sufficient supply of working capital to cover the gap between income and expenditures, since the latter often outpaces the former. This effort requires accurate, compulsive record keeping and timely (usually monthly) updating of payables (what the firm owes) and receivables (what is owed the firm).

Another kind of computing cited in table 9.1 relates to the many quantitative aspects of project design: preliminary estimates of construction costs; construction bids; the footages and dimensions of programmed spaces and areas in buildings; zoning, site, and building code parameters (area, yard dimensions, building sizes and heights, occupancy, fire egress); quantities, sizes, and costs of components specified; building dimensions; and, in engineering design, types and magnitudes of loads imposed on engineered systems (structural loads, heating and air conditioning loads, ventilation requirements, water and sewer demand, electrical loads, excavation quantities for cut and fill, and others). Although consulting engineers may undertake the detailed computational analyses required, the architect may determine relevant loading conditions and perform preliminary calculations. In simple construction, such as individual residences, architects often do their own structural design "accounting" using reference tables and simple formulas.

Construction cost estimating is done by architects with varying degrees of reliability. On the one hand, clients expect architects to be knowledgeable about building costs, to be able to predict with some accuracy how much any project will cost to construct (excluding the costs of land, financing, fees, and furnishings). On the other hand, most general contractors know that a project's cost can never be pinpointed accurately until the construction documents are completed, and they are usually skeptical about cost estimates done by architects.

Contractors' detailed bids are based on exacting quantity surveys of construction drawings, a process in which estimators compute the quantity and cost of installing each and every item needed to construct the project as designed. Since estimates are needed before working drawings are finished, and even before design is begun, what can architects and owner/clients do? They use comparables. If a comparison can be made between the project being designed and other similar projects whose costs are known, then a somewhat realistic estimate can be projected.

Of course, to ensure comparability, the architect must consider the geographic location, size, complexity, quality, type, and time of construction of the comparable projects. Allowances must be made for inflation if data are not very recent. Most comparable cost data are expressed in dollars per square foot of enclosed building floor area, although cost figures may also be stated for other units of building size (such as volume). Needless to say, such estimates, no matter how carefully made, are always intelligent guesses. Rarely are any two project designs or sites wholly comparable, and there are always enough special conditions to introduce large margins for error.

Architects' optimism contributes additional error in preliminary estimating, as architects are notoriously consistent in underestimating the ultimate costs of their designs. This accounts for their reluctance to guarantee a construction cost as part of their agreement with clients. If they did, they would often be obliged to redesign and redraw their projects, going bankrupt in the process. Prudent architects do their best to predict construction costs conservatively, hoping to look good when the bids come in at or below their estimates. At the same time prudent clients should always add a healthy contingency to architects' estimates, no matter how conservative. It's been said that any good architect wasn't trying hard enough if the project designed was bid within budget.

Model Making

Familiar to all architectural students and apprentice architects is the activity of model building. Few good architects would design a project of any size or consequence without making one or more scale models, usually during the schematic and design development phases, as mentioned before. Like drafting, model making is labor intensive, and the amount of time required depends on the complexity of the design and the overall size of the model. Also like drawing some architects do it better or more quickly than others. Some architects love to build models, whereas others dislike it intensely.

Anyone who enjoys using his or her hands, who can derive inherent pleasure from crafting something carefully and beautifully, will probably be a good model maker. Of course, if one is overly laborious and painstaking, to the point of never finishing, then the love of craft may be superseded by the boss's concerns for time and money. No matter how fast or careful, model builders must have patience, steady eyes and hands, a concern for edges and joints, and an instinct for materials.

There is great joy in constructing a model of a design you have created, for models can most closely approximate three-dimensional reality. And there can be joy in doing a model for a design you like, but created by someone else. But there is little joy in making models of projects whose design you dislike or cannot respect. Unfortunately many a young architect has been obliged to labor for what seems an eternity, building models of unloved buildings. This is a rut to be avoided in the road to practice.

Client Contact

Architects not in senior positions in firms frequently complain that they never get to meet or work directly with the firm's clients. There may be several reasons for this. First, they may be too junior in the hierarchy to attend client meetings, perhaps already overcrowded by the presence of a senior partner, a design partner, a project manager, and a job captain. Second, they may be perceived to be (how can I put it?) unpresentable. The boss may think that a particular architect-employee speaks poorly or inappropriately, dresses offensively, or otherwise poses the risk of embarrassment. He or she tolerates the employee for other purposes. Third, some clients prefer to meet only with the nominal head of the firm, notwithstanding the sometimes minimal role played by that principal in carrying out the project. Fourth, there may exist intraoffice jealousies, rivalries, and resentments between individuals. One architect may feel threatened or intimidated by another, perhaps because of differences in skills, talents, or personality. However, in the case of small offices or project teams, everyone will inevitably interact with clients . . . and with all other participants as well.

Government Approvals

Another subroutine in the day-to-day life of the architect worthy of elaboration is the struggle with government-approving agencies. A portion of every architect's time is devoted to persuading local building and zoning departments, zoning appeals boards, design review panels, or planning commissions that a proposed design is lawful, that it conforms to all of the confusing and often conflicting regulations promulgated by government agencies, and that it is in the public interest. To accomplish this, architects must submit design drawings for review to each appropriate agency, explaining and justifying them to officials and technical staff, many of whom claim that they are overworked and underpaid. Moreover it is not unusual for two officials to offer more than one interpretation of a single regulation.

When beginning to design a project, responsible architects search through applicable building codes for those requirements and standards that apply to the project being designed. Yet that is never sufficient to ensure code compliance, which is why some architects make an effort at getting to know certain agency officials so well. Dealing with them, as with clients and contractors, demands negotiating tactics and diplomacy, flexibility and firmness at the same time.

Relief comes with final approvals, but frustration can occur when building permits are applied for, and the architect learns that despite reading the codes and conferring endlessly with officials, the permit is denied or delayed because of failure to comply 100 percent with the regulations. Or worse, criteria have changed since last checked. This bit of news may precipitate a fast trip to the permit office with pencils and paper in hand, where the architect instantly modifies the permit set of drawings while trying to maintain a smile. Remember that reviewers of any kind feel obliged to find something wrong, always, lest their jobs or purpose be challenged.

Consultants and Coordination

Collaboration, not confrontation, is the way architects can and should work with engineering and other consultants. Ideally engineering consultants should join the project design effort not long after the architect's work has started. Once schematic design is under way or completed, engineers can study the architect's design concept and begin to formulate appropriate engineering strategies, advising the architect accordingly. As design development moves forward, preliminary engineering drawings may be started. During the construction documents phase, all of the drawings and specifications—architectural and engineering—must be prepared and, most critically, coordinated. The coordination process is crucial because the work of each participant affects the work of all the others. Normally the project architect or job captain is responsible for coordination, accomplished by periodic meetings and telephone conversations between architects and engineers and by transmitting memoranda and drawings back and forth between offices for cross-checking.

The coordination challenge can be staggering. Inside any building there are places where elements of structure (such as beams or columns), ductwork, pipes, conduits (such as electrical and telephone), and walls all want to occupy roughly the same space at the same time, an obvious impossibility. Yet each element is a necessary component of a necessary system contributing to the building as a whole, and many of these elements are shown in more than one drawing. Thus the coordinating architect's job is to visualize and draw very carefully such conditions, like three-dimensional maps, to avoid conflicts and to show elements of the design consistently. If conflicts slip through, they are usually discovered when the condition is encountered by the contractor in the field. The contractor may then stop work, alert everyone, request a solution, and mentally pocket the extra funds he's entitled to claim for the extra work caused by the coordination error. In turn the client may claim payment from the architect or engineer.

Computers and Design

Computer-aided drafting systems can be useful in expediting repetitive or standardized pieces of the design process—drawing and storing in memory standard details, schedules, components, and layouts. But they will not completely replace the knowledgeable architect/draftsperson who must research, study, evaluate, coordinate, and draw the many atypical design conditions and options present in every project. In fact the computer's unmatched ability to handle volumes of data and standardized drawing of standard items should permit architects to design more thoroughly than in the past, when reuse of old design solutions or the continuation of obsolete assumptions had so often resulted in poor construction or building performance.

Computer-aided design and drawing are not limited to contract documents. The ability of computer graphics systems to draw and reproduce quickly designs described by the architect to the machine allows the designer to explore many more alternative architectural concepts. There are graphics programs that will produce perspective views from any vantage point, interior or exterior, add color, simulate movement around or within an environment, and change drawing scales at will, almost instantaneously. There is software for generating space programs and functional diagrams, for doing cost analyses, and for handling many aspects of engineering design.

The same computer is available for word processing, creating standardized contract documents, specifications and letters, maintaining mailing and other lists, and bookkeeping and accounting. There is little question that within a few years, most architects in practice will be using office computers for these and other purposes not yet envisioned. Fortunately most of these machines and related software are sufficiently "user friendly" that architects, young or old, need not contemplate this trend with anxiety.

Construction Services

Finally, let us look at the routines of construction phase services and activities. Highlighted earlier, they contrast sharply with all previous phases. During construction of a project, architects spend most of their time doing one of three things: (1) visiting the job site to make inspections or attend on-site meetings with the contractor, owner/client, subcontractors, engineers, inspectors, or suppliers; (2) reviewing shop drawings, usually in the office, submitted by the contractor and subcontractors; (3) writing reports, memoranda, certifications for payment, and letters to the owner/client, contractor, government agencies, lenders, or file.

The third activity was discussed before. The first is characterized by frequent scheduled and unscheduled trips to and from the site, which can be very close or very far; by oceans of mud or debris at the site, necessitating ownership of at least one pair of very good, high, waterproof boots and a hard hat which many architects keep at the ready in their car; by exposure to the risks of rain, snow, ice, heat, cold, and projecting rusty nails; by inevitable disputes or shouting matches between parties before, during, or after job site meetings; by the thankless task of having to tell the construction superintendent that work in place will have to be torn out and redone at the contractor's expense; by the recurring feeling of being persona non grata; and, perhaps most memorably, by the elation or disappointment felt when your design, previously realized only on paper, is seen in fully constructed form for the first time.

Many architects find the second activity, reviewing and checking shop drawings, to be one of the most boring and tedious of all the architect's jobs. A shop drawing is a detailed drawing prepared by the fabricator of some part of the building—such as steel reinforcing or structural members, cabinetry, special equipment installations, railings, curtain wall assemblies—and supposedly based on the architect's design drawings. The shop drawing, not the architect's drawing, is used to manufacture the components to be furnished and installed by the contractor. Shop drawings are sent to the architect because both the fabricator and the contractor want to be sure that what is made complies with the design and will fit into the building. If it does not comply, then the architect's responsibility, after uncovering the discrepancies, is to alert the contractor by disapproving the submitted shop drawing. Ordinarily the architect does this by marking on the shop drawing (in red) and requesting a resubmittal.

In large projects there can be hundreds of shop drawings with thousands of dimensions and many opportunities for error. Therefore you can imagine what it might be like to process and scrutinize every one of these drawings. They are supposed to be submitted well in advance of the time when installation is scheduled, but sometimes this doesn't happen. Contractors often dump loads of shop drawings in the architect's lap over a short period of time, only to claim later that the completion of construction was delayed because the architect was slow or late in

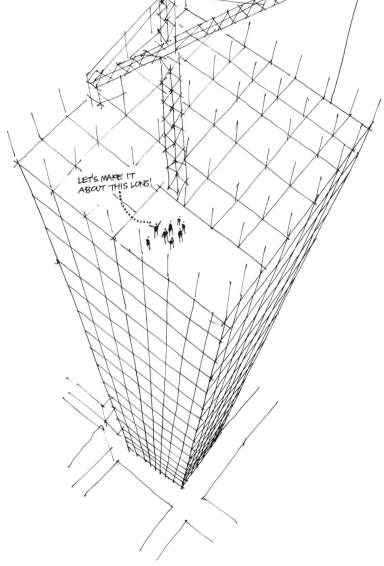

Architect issuing instructions during progress meeting at the construction site.

reviewing them. In the best of circumstances shop drawings should be submitted many weeks ahead of installation in order to give both architect and fabricator enough time to correct, coordinate, fabricate, and deliver.

Organization within Architectural Firms

An architectural firm may be comprised of one, ten or a hundred architects. Large firms may also include engineers and cost estimators, with secretaries, bookkeepers, and other administrative assistants making up the support staff. But how are firms structured so that each member of the firm knows where he or she is in the hierarchy or pecking order?

Size of firm is a big factor in determining firm structure. A one person firm poses no problem, since that one person plays all roles. Once there are two or more people, however, things become much more complex, and firms with more than five or six people border on becoming institutions. Legally, most firms are either sole proprietorships, owned entirely by a single individual, or partnerships of two or more owners. There can be any number of partners. Firm owners, be they sole proprietors or partners, are entitled to the firm's profits, but they also assume responsibility for the firm's losses and liabilities. Owners set firm policy, make final decisions, hire and fire personnel, and enjoy other benefits of business ownership.

Some states allow architectural firms to be incorporated, but the individual architects who own the firm's stock and direct its affairs are still held liable as individuals for professional negligence in the firm's work. Incorporation offers other benefits related to deferral of income for pensions and retirement, as well as protection from nonprofessional business liabilities. Otherwise, they operate much like partnerships. In all forms of organization the architects who own the firm must provide the financing necessary to start and sustain operations.

Most firms structure themselves internally in two ways: by rank and by function. Rank-structured firms are headed by one or several senior partners, perhaps founders of the firm. Below them are other partners who play differing functional roles within the firm. Then come associates, experienced staff members who may share in part of the firm's profits but who are not owners of the firm. Finally comes the professional staff, usually the youngest members of the firm. In large offices they populate the drafting rooms and do most of the drawing. Many of them are unregistered apprentices, only a few years out of school. In smaller firms such ranking is less noticed, although there are still employers and employees.

Of greater interest here is the functional structure of architectural firms. From the foregoing discussions we can see that there are two broad areas of activity—firm operations and project operations. Firm operations such as marketing and promotion, personnel management, and financial management are normally in the hands of senior partners assisted by appropriate staff members. These partners are primarily responsible for obtaining the firm's commissions, representing the firm to the outside world, and overseeing the general internal management of the firm.

Project operations, the set of activities that directly generates the firm's income and most of its expenses, are often characterized by a project team approach. The team may vary in size with each new phase, or one person may play more than one position on the team. A typical team structure would consist of the following players:

Partner in charge   Usually a senior partner who may have been instrumental in marketing, making contact with the client and bringing in the commission; he or she may not spend much time turning out the work itself, acting primarily as a front person.

Project designer/architect   A partner or associate who takes prime responsibility for the conceptual design of the project, the lead author of the work; may also be the partner in charge.

Job captain/project manager   Usually an experienced associate, who may also be the primary designer, responsible for managing the day-to-day flow of work on the project, including coordination with consultants, maintenance of project records and correspondence, checking of drawings and specifications, and supervision of drafting; may also do drafting.

Architectural draftsperson/designer   The professional who does most of the labor-intensive drawings, lettering, model building, running of prints, and, occasionally, brewing of coffee; he or she may get to meet clients, hassle with contractors and building department officials, and, if talented, do schematic design work.

Secretary and/or bookkeeper   In some ways the most important members of any business organization of any size, they are frequently the only people in the office who know how much money is in the bank, who works for the firm, where everything is located (especially if it's in a filing cabinet), who is supposed to meet with who (and when and where), and what everybody earns; they are truly indispensable, like the client getters.

Project teams may also be created through departmentalization within larger offices. Thus there may be a design group, a production (contract documents) group, a specifications group, an interiors group, a cost-estimating group, and a construction administration group. Each group or department may be headed by a partner responsible for the management of his or her department's activities. This means that he or she may be supervising work on several projects at any one time. In A/E firms the engineering departments may also be large; some have more engineers than architects and would be more correctly labeled E/A firms. Departmentalized firms may be very efficient in producing work quickly because of specialization, but they may also create artificial barriers and competition between departments. I suspect that most young architects prefer the team approach, since working on a project team in a big firm can feel like working in a little firm.

The Goals of Architectural Firms

To bring this chapter to a conclusion and lead you to the next, it seems appropriate to discuss briefly the various goals firms pursue, either explicitly or implicitly. Explicit firm goals are rarely stated anywhere outside of firm brochures, most of which promise great design done within budget, on schedule, efficiently, effectively, and for reasonable cost. The implicit goals are more telling and are evidenced by the kind of work a firm does rather than by what it says it does.

With this in mind we can generally categorize goals as follows:

1. *Quality* of *design* over all else.
2. *Design innovation* over all else.
3. *Professional reputation* and *fame* over all else.
4. *Service* to the *client* over all else.
5. *Service* to the *community* and *public* over all else.
6. *Business volume* and *profit* over all else.

These goals are not mutually exclusive. A firm could pursue any or all of them. But most firms tend to develop goal structures that dominate their approach to practice and contribute to their image and reputation. The newly graduated architect should be sensitive to the biases of firms where employment might be sought, for such biases can be easily transmitted.

One goal, one bias, is universally shared by virtually all architects in practice . . . to be hired by a client to design a building. Achieving this objective is the subject of the next chapter.

10

How Architects Get Work

Several times a year I receive pamphlets from the AIA or other organizations typically entitled "Marketing Your Architectural Services." Such pamphlets are sent to architects inviting them to attend seminars or workshops on market research, sniffing out new business, promotion, public relations, client relationships, and presentation techniques.

Until recently marketing was rarely addressed or acknowledged so explicitly by the architectural profession. In fact many professionals would argue that marketing is unprofessional, an activity reserved for those who engage in trade, the buying and selling of products, and not for those who render professional services. Actively marketing services conjured up visions of commercial advertising, self-promotion, exaggerated claims, unfair competitive practices, and even "specials" and "discounts." Yet architects have always been naturally competitive, realizing that if they just sat back, relaxed, and waited for new clients to call, they might very well starve to death.

In today's extremely competitive climate, getting work has become so time-consuming and critical an activity in architectural practice that anyone considering a career in architecture must at least be aware of marketing methods and goals. We will examine the reasons clients select architects, how they select them, and what architects do to improve their chances of being selected.

Getting the First Job

The day you look for your first job as a draftsperson in an architectural office is your first day marketing. You are selling yourself and the services you can provide. From your perspective the architectural firm is your client. In most cases the best strategy is to make an overall, favorable impression. Somehow you want the firm to remember you rather than others interviewed, to like your portfolio of work more than others, to feel more comfortable and confident about you in comparison to other job applicants. You want to look good, and you want your "client" to feel certain that you can and will do the best job possible.

This certainly sounds like sales pitching. It is! And as so often mentioned in this book, the ability to persuade other people to "buy" your talent and ideas can be no less essential than the ability to draw. Effectively selling yourself and your services requires two complementary conditions: you must have something to sell, on the one hand, and there must be a demand, a need, a market, on the other.

For that first office job, getting hired can be tough. You believe you have something to sell, the skills acquired in school, but you quickly learn that prospective employers want both skills *and* experience. You lack the latter. How, you wonder, can one ever get that first job if only experienced architects are employable? To gain experience, one must get that first job. It can seem like a vicious circle—a "Catch 22" phenomenon—but eventually most find that first job. They find a job because a firm decides it needs help, often immediately, and believes the applicant to be ready, willing, able, and, above all, available. In fact for many young architects seeking work, the first job or two is frequently the result of being in the right place at the right time. Luck and timing are always factors in the marketing process, no matter how much talent is offered.

Economic Conditions

Both individual, neophyte architects and architectural firms face the same problem in getting work, in addition to competition—the uncertainty and variability of the marketplace. Jobs with firms exist only when firms have projects to work on, and projects depend on many people and forces beyond the control of the architect. General economic conditions, worldwide and nationally, and local economic circumstances greatly affect building activity and consequently the employment of architects. When credit is available and inexpensive, prices stable, and optimism high, society builds. But when money is tight and recession occurs, building slows down. Understandably architects are bellwethers, sensing shifts in building mood early in the building process through the mood shifts of clients, contractors, lenders, and other building industry participants. When it's boom or bust for the country, it is generally boom or bust for architects.

Territory

Architects' markets are geographic and territorial. Most of us make locational decisions before any other major decisions regarding our careers, and firms must do likewise, at least until they achieve regional, national, or international status. Thus architects must decide where to be—in what state, city, and neighborhood—and where to build, which is not limited to only that area immediately surrounding their offices. Selecting one's market territory may be influenced by factors such as potential for population and economic growth, preferences for climate and natural environment, urban amenities, exurban amenities, lack of competition, social or business affiliations, and familial needs. As you can see, some of these factors have to do with the market itself, whereas others have to do with the personal desires of the architect.

Market territories can be very small or virtually unlimited in size. Most architectural firms concentrate on local markets, rooting themselves in towns, counties, or cities and doing most of their projects within these local jurisdictions, their home "turfs." Cities like Boston, Washington, D.C., and San Francisco are urban metropolitan areas comprised of many jurisdictions, so that architects' practices, though still considered local, may cross multiple political boundaries.

Some architectural firms, as they grow and become better known, expand their territory for building to include entire states and regions—east coast, west coast, midwest, and sunbelt are familiar regions. A few architects and architectural firms attain sufficient reputations and stature to enjoy national and international market territories, independent totally of where their offices are located. Their projects may be anywhere in the country or overseas. Their practices may be unaffected by localized market conditions, and they may not even compete for local work unless it has, in their view, national or international significance.

Not all firms whose markets are geographically broad are famous and well known. There are several large architectural/engineering firms that do specialized projects all over the world, often involving sophisticated technologies and equipment and requiring many employees to carry out the work. Yet these firms' names are not household words, either within or outside of the architectural profession. They provide services mostly to industry, domestic and foreign government agencies, and real estate developers. Much of their work, though large and complex in scope, receives little media attention. But they too are not overly dependent on local markets.

Types of Markets

Architects spend a lot of time thinking about the type of market or client they want to pursue. Not only must they pick their territory, they must also decide on the kinds of projects they want to do within that territory. They may be generalist architects, going after any and all work that comes along and in which they are interested. They may choose to specialize in certain types and sizes of projects if they have a choice, such as single residences, multifamily housing, office buildings and other commercial structures, health care facilities, educational buildings, or hotels. They may seek only prestigious, high-budget, institutional commissions, such as museums, corporate headquarters, university buildings, or city halls. Or they may stick to the opposite end of the cost-status spectrum, doing only tight-budget, bread-and-butter projects such as highway strip shopping centers, low-rent offices and warehouses, factory structures, and moderate-income housing. Still others specialize in renovation, remodeling, and historic preservation regardless of project use or type.

If given the choice, most architects would probably prefer that (1) their market territory be national or international, as well as local, and (2) their projects be of all types, so long as they are high budget, visible, and prestigious. Obviously, this is hard to achieve. In fact most architects end up doing what they do for circumstantial reasons. They locate, begin practice, and establish reputations based partly on the kind of work that first comes in and gets built. This early work contributes to the making of a track record and reputation, the buildup of experience that employers and clients look for. Once on a track, it is difficult to get off, though not impossible with some luck and much effort.

Selecting Architects for Projects

Why and how do clients select architects? The rest of this chapter answers this question in two ways. First, we will see what clients look for, already hinted at earlier. Then we will explore the specific actions architects take to make themselves known, loved, and chosen.

In 1977, working with students in a course on professional practice, I wrote a paper ("An Assessment of Architectural Practice," published by the University of Maryland School of Architecture) in which we tried to pinpoint reasons why clients choose architects. Our conclusions were based on a limited survey in Maryland conducted by the students, who submitted questionnaires to both architects and nonarchitects. Quoting directly from the document: "survey respondents, including architects, were asked to identify the most important considerations in choosing an architect. Following are the frequencies of response:

Design talent and creativity	50
Prior experience in similar work	33
Organization and management skills	29
Knowledge of practical aspects of building	25
Fees (cost of services)	15
Reputation	6

It is interesting to note that architects, when asked to rank those architectural products which 'sell' best, or are most in demand gave highest ranking to 'functional design,' 'competitive fees and 'economy/cost control,' and lowest ranking to building image,' 'aesthetics,' and 'innovation/novelty.' "

There are of course other factors, and other results would be obtained depending on the persons interviewed. However, we can generalize and, I hope, cover most of the client's viewpoint. With no particular ranking, consider the following criteria for selection:

1. *Reputation* as to credentials and professional experience.
2. *Reputation* as to creativity, inventiveness, style.
3. *Reputation* as to personal qualities, integrity.
4. *Reputation* as to performance, to meeting client goals.
5. *Reputation* as to fees, financial arrangements.
6. *Rapport* with client and others.
7. *Convenience* as to location and accessibility.

Note that, except for items 6 and 7, these criteria are all stated as reputations. Reputation implies what one is known for, how one is seen by others. Use of the word intentionally suggests that a client, after selecting and working with a particular architect, may conclude that some aspects of the architect's reputation were unfounded. Nevertheless, in selecting an architect, it's the client's perception of reputation that matters.

Although some of these criteria are self-explanatory, several merit further explanation. Take number 2, for example. Many clients are keenly interested in choosing an architect who is reputed to be not only creative and imaginative in design but who also does work considered to be in fashion or avant garde. They shop for specific styles by scrutinizing architectural firms' recent projects and verifying their aesthetic track records.

Item 4, performance, is critical to many clients. They look for architects who meet deadlines, whose projects are buildable within budget limitations, whose offices are neat and smoothly managed, and who can provide a long list of satisfied customers. This is closely related to criteria 6 and 7. For almost all clients good rapport with an architect is a necessity. They ask themselves: Can we communicate with each other? Does this architect understand and sympathize with our needs and problems? Are we comfortable working closely together? Do we share the same values regarding the project? Will we ever see the senior partner again?

Unfortunately some clients associate firm size with ability to perform, assuming that only big firms can do big projects. Big firms do not necessarily perform better than small firms, although they clearly have substantial marketing advantages. Regardless of firm size it is the project team that counts, and the team available in a small firm may be as large and capable as the team assigned by a large firm. Indeed, one advantage of small firms is that more of the work is likely to be done by the firm's principals and senior staff, perhaps even with more care, since such projects are so few and far between for smaller offices.

Matters relating to criterion 5 may be the stickiest. The ideal client, as stated earlier, is one willing to pay whatever it costs to do the job right, but almost all clients are cost conscious to some degree, and for many the cost of architectural services may be a primary factor in selecting an architect. Three forces act upon fee negotiations. Force one is what the client believes to be an affordable fee. Force two is what the architect believes to be an adequate fee. Force three is what the so-called market fee appears to be, that is, what the perceived competition would charge. Force one fees are generally *below* force three fees, while force two fees are generally *above.* Persuading clients to pay fair and adequate fees is not easy in this situation. Occasionally failure to agree on fees can cost architects the job, since clients can always find architects who will do the work for less money.

In addition to shopping for fee bargains, clients may also want to negotiate terms for payment of fees that are unfavorable to the architect's cash flow. Thus the total amount of the fee could pose less difficulty than how or when the fees are paid. Clients sometimes ask architects to defer receiving payment until some future date or to accept a note (IOU) or ownership interest in the project.

Nevertheless, architects who are skillful negotiators can overcome such difficulties by convincing clients that, in truth, one gets what one pays for. This requires taking time to show the client precisely what must be done to execute the project correctly, completely, and creatively. Time and cost allocations must be shown in detail so that the client understands how and why the proposed fees have been calculated. Each step in the design and construction process must be identified and explained. Once the client comprehends the scope of work and the architect's cash flow requirements, and if he or she believes that the architect is otherwise the right choice for the project, then architect and client can reach agreement, even knowing that there are other firms who would work for less.

Unfortunately governmental clients are frequently the exception, since they may be required by statute always to choose architects who offer services for the lowest fees and who appear to be qualified. For this reason many of the best architects do little or no government projects, and those who do often find that they lose money or break even doing government work. But such work can pay the rent and keep the staff busy while partners look for more stimulating and lucrative commissions.

Sadly, a few architects, in an effort to secure commissions, have been tempted to make kickback arrangements, whereby a portion of the architect's fee, after being paid, is returned "under the table" or is "contributed" to an appropriately designated recipient. Tragically it is easy to imagine a hungry, ambitious architect agreeing to such terms with a client, or offering cut-rate services, when the wolf is at the door and a new commission is pending.

It must now be evident that architects cannot be passive practitioners in today's world. For better or worse, we cannot behave like sellers in a sellers' market. We cannot assume, like doctors or lawyers, that a combination of aptitude, talent, good credentials, and the right "start" will lead inevitably to success and an ample supply of work. We must go and get it, since all of our colleagues do likewise.

It must also be evident that since reputation counts for so much, getting work must mean getting *known*. Becoming and being known as an architect achieves the same purpose as it does for McDonald's or Mercedes-Benz . . . name recognition and product reputation. Architects are forced to find ways to promote themselves, to advertise their work and their ideas, to let clients know who they are. As we shall see, some architects do this overtly, some in more subtle ways. Some efforts verge on commercial advertising, whereas others lead more indirectly to notoriety and repute. However, any one of the activities described here can in some fashion contribute to making an architect known and in turn help to get work. Remember too that not all architects engage in all of these activities. Indeed, some are thought to be unprofessional, or even unethical, by many architects.

The Direct Approach

1. Follow project leads; call on and cultivate prospective clients; read newspapers, magazines, journals, government and business publications, looking for items that advertise or mention future or pending projects; write letters expressing interest to prospective clients.

2. Publish and distribute firm brochures, illustrating the firm's work, capabilities, and qualifications; such brochures must be updated periodically and are sometimes tailored to appeal to certain types of clients; always mention awards, special project features, and prestigious client references.

3. Issue press releases to local newspapers or national journals, announcing "news" such as awards received, new projects, or changes in address or personnel.

4. Enter design competitions, if time and finances permit; there are always several local, regional, national, and international competitions in progress at any given time, and although the chances of winning may be remote, you can have fun doing them—and they can be added to your brochure, portfolio, or resumé.

5. Advertise in the media, considered unethical until recently; now, although still rare, paid commercial advertising in newspapers, magazines, journals, and on radio and television is perfectly legal and, according to the AIA, ethical; this approach remains relatively untested and, for many, distasteful.

The Indirect Approach

The indirect approach to promoting oneself or one's firm is the most common. Rather than focusing directly on a prospective client or market, architects can enhance name recognition and reputation through activities that are noncommercial, more subtle, and perhaps more effective than the direct approach, ways that many deem to be more professional than simply asking someone to hire them.

1. Be socially active; entertain people, especially those who might be potential clients or who might refer clients to you; memberships and active participation in appropriate clubs may prove fruitful.

2. Join and participate in various civic, business, and professional organizations; the architect can contribute useful advice and meet many influential people in a community.

3. Publish work, usually finished projects, in local, regional, or national media such as newspapers and professional journals; hometown newspaper articles can have the same effect as advertising, and exposure in professional journals builds one's reputation among colleagues.

4. Give lectures and speeches to local audiences, to schools, or at conferences; participation in seminars, workshops, and other educational programs also contributes to furthering name recognition and reputation.

5. Submit projects to win awards in local, regional, and national awards competition programs, most of which are for design; this requires properly documenting (photos, slides, presentation drawings) and submitting one's work on a fairly regular basis; expect recognition to be periodic, since work awarded depends largely on the tastes and moods of design awards juries; ideally publicize such awards (press releases) when possible.

6. Write about architecture, either articles or books; any subject will do if someone will publish it, although controversial subjects and personal manifestos seem to attract the most attention.

7. Be written about if you have done something significant or have become someone sufficiently interesting; being the subject of someone else's writing, even objective criticism, can establish you as a "famous" person in the eyes of the reading public and among many reading architects; this is accomplished most readily when you have friends in the media, particularly architectural journalists.

Self-promotion by architects is easiest when their work is news-worthy or when they become so well established that anything they do or advocate gains an audience. Becoming recognized, respected, and famous is difficult for those who do only competent work and almost impossible for those who do poor or uninteresting work. But it may also be difficult if they make no effort explicitly to promote themselves using the approaches outlined here. Today it is not enough to just be good at what you do, to be an expert or a great talent. Something more is needed. You must now be willing to tell the world what you can do.

Assuming that an architectural firm has established itself and enjoys some kind of positive reputation, it must still face the reality of stiff competition, since there will typically be many firms available and qualified for any given project at any given time. This means that at some point, firms must use the direct approach to obtain commissions, no matter how successful they have been utilizing the indirect approach. How, then, do clients and architects finally get together?

Our 1977 survey addressed this question specifically.

Generally, architects are selected to do a single project. Unlike doctors, lawyers, or accountants who usually have continuing relationships with clients over extended time periods, the architect may do only one project for a particular client. If hired again by the same client, it is nevertheless on a project-by-project basis. Clients find and select architects . . .

through personal contact, either social or professional;

through referral, based on reputation and qualifications;

through client-sponsored competitions based on professional and other qualifications;

through client-sponsored competitions based on fees;

through client-sponsored design competitions.

Indeed, architectural firms get most of their leads through referrals and personal contacts. But they must still sell themselves after meeting the prospective client.

The Interview

Skill is required to meet, woo, and sign a client, and it must be applied in that most critical of architect/client encounters, the *interview*, of which there can be more than one for a single commission. An interview is like a first date; initial impressions are lasting and powerful. The architect, when the appropriate moment arrives, must make his or her move to enthrall and captivate. The romancing is done with both words and images, usually projected in color by 35mm carousel slide projectors and accompanied by well-composed, slickly printed brochures. Architects sometimes refer to this as their "dog and pony show."

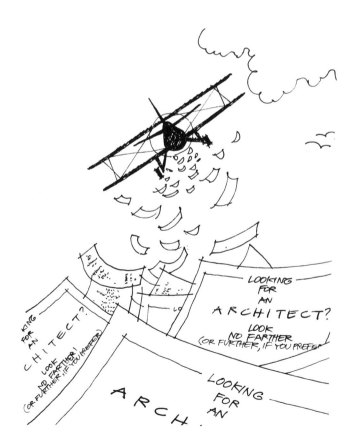

Having captured a prospective client's attention, architects must convince the client that they alone possess the unique qualities sought, and that their future working relationship will be ideal. In addition to past work, they must demonstrate their competencies by showing qualifications of personnel, management strategies (if any), and philosophical approach. Fees for services will usually be the last item of negotiation, and these may be discussed in detail only after the architect has made a definitive, written proposal.

Joint Ventures

To compete more effectively, architectural firms sometimes form joint ventures with other architectural firms, or with engineering firms. A joint venture is a temporary partnership between two or more firms created specifically for the purpose of carrying out a specific project; otherwise, the firms continue to conduct business as separate entities. Joint venturing can expand geographic coverage and broaden expertise. It's a marriage of convenience, transforming small firms into big firms and big firms into bigger firms. Boston firms can become Chicago firms, or office-building firms can become hospital firms. Occasionally joint ventures result when clients want a "design-oriented" firm to team up with a "nuts-and-bolts" firm. In this instance, the former normally takes responsibility for the schematic and design development phases of architectural services, whereas the latter prepares construction documents and oversees construction.

Architects as Contractors and Developers

In recent years architects have increasingly turned toward "design-build" and "design-develop" modes of survival. In the design-build mode, architects wear two hats: they act as both designers and contractors, offering a bigger package of services to clients. Most design-build architects limit themselves to small projects, primarily residential (single houses or multifamily housing, and rehabilitation) and small-scale commercial projects.

Merging the architectural and contracting functions can be appealing for both architects and clients, but there can also be financial risks for both. And a potential conflict of interest exists for 'the architect because, although the client seeks the most and the best (within the budget) from the architect and contractor, the contractor's objective is usually to build the architect's design at the least possible cost, an incentive to cut corners and compromise quality. If the architect plays both roles, there is no mediator between the owner/client's and the contractor's interests. Ultimately the outcome of design-build relationships depends on the integrity of the architect.

Being one's own client can be very appealing. For young architects the architect-as-developer strategy represents a potentially rewarding but risky means for getting work. Not only can practicing architects earn significant development profits as developers, but also they can exercise more control over the final design product, within the limits of budgets and marketability. Again most development forays by architects have been into housing or small commercial projects. The architect, often joined by other investment partners, carries out essentially all of the functions of the real estate developer—land acquisition, equity and debt financing, construction, and marketing—in addition to the design functions of the architect.

Projects developed by architects are no more likely to succeed than to fail economically. However, relatively few actively practicing architects have been both successful developers and successful architects. A notable exception, in a class by himself, is John Portman, the Atlanta architect best known for his hotel-and-atria ventures in many major U.S. cities. What many architect-developers have found is that designing projects is not at all the same as developing projects. Each requires altogether different expertise, interests, psychic energy, business skills, and attitudes. Each entails very different risks and requires different kinds of stomach linings. Nevertheless, architects will always be tempted by the perceived liberty of designing for themselves.

Design Competitions

Some architects believe that design competitions are one of the fairest methods for selecting architects. Other architects hold the opposite view. The former believe that open competitions offer small firms, or relatively undiscovered architects, the opportunity to "score" quickly and emphatically, to make their mark and gain recognition against overwhelming odds and to win monetary prizes and significant design commissions. They further argue that design competitions bring out the best designers and stimulate the most creative, innovative design thinking, bringing forth proposals that the average or nonchalant architect, working with a conservative client, might never dream of.

Competition cynics or opponents claim that competitions are inherently unfair because the outcomes often reflect the biases of the jury who selects the winners, usually for stylistic reasons, while failing to address and grapple with the needs or tastes of the client and project users. They claim that competitions favor either architectural firms with ample financial and staff resources, allowing such firms a potential edge in presentation, or, conversely, firms whose work load is slack. Architects who are busy may have difficulty finding sufficient time to undertake competitions without compromising both the competition effort and their efforts on behalf of their regular, fee-paying clients. Another objection raised by architects is that many competitions are poorly managed by sponsors, some of whom are seen to be taking advantage of architects' willingness to go for the brass ring, their purpose being to obtain lots of design ideas at minimal cost.

A very small percentage of all projects designed by architects are the result of open design competitions. Frequently winning designs are never executed, and monetary prizes rarely cover the time costs incurred by the successful competitors. When both a prize and a commission are awarded, the winning architect may still suffer financial loss or, as sometimes occurs, may be "excused" from completing the work for technical, economic, or political reasons, only to have his or her design altered and executed by someone else. And in many competitions, vital interaction between architect and client during the formative phases of design is missing.

Ultimately design competitions, as a method for getting work, are a long shot for almost all architects in practice. Competition sponsors and the projects they build may well benefit from the profusion of ideas and the investment of thousands of hours accumulated by all of the losing competition entrants, who, after their costly search for success and recognition, may end up with feelings of frustration, envy, sour grapes, and resentment, no matter how much fun was had participating. But, to be a winner . . . !

Free Services

One last marketing tactic is worth noting: doing work at no cost to the client. For many years the AIA and the profession in general condemned the practice of furnishing prospective clients with free sketches, designs, or other services without fair compensation. To do so was considered unprofessional and unfair. Yet this occurs frequently. It is the architect's loss leader, the come-on for subsequent procurement by the client. But there is nothing illegal about providing free services—unethical perhaps but not illegal. Said Jerome Cooper FAIA at the 1976 AIA convention in Philadelphia:

The prohibition against providing "free sketches" is contained in Article 8 and Article 12 of the present (ethical) standards. I do not need to dwell unduly on the conditions that would exist in this profession but for this prohibition . . . It was precisely these conditions which existed in our profession prior to 1909 that called into being the first Cannon of Ethics. Up until that time, the Federal Government as well as many others were receiving free sketch proposals from architects on projects they were contemplating—competitions without compensation.

Small firms with limited resources cannot long compete with large firms and larger resources in this arena. What we will have created is an environment of "unfair competition." Let us make no mistake about this—this is not a scenario for the "survival of the fittest and most capable"—this is a scenario for the "survival of the richest."

Let's conclude this chapter with these observations made in our 1977 study; they are still timely:

1. Getting work is becoming an ever-larger and rapidly expanding part of the practicing architect's efforts.

2. Getting work is becoming increasingly costly for architects.

3. The chances of being selected for a project are decreasing as competition quantitatively increases.

4. The process by which some architects find clients and clients select architects may be accidental, arbitrary, inequitable, or even unethical.

5. Architects' marketing techniques are becoming less "professional" and more "commercial" in nature, with the practice of architecture being transformed into the business of architecture.

Many architects voice regret over the transformation of architectural practice. But they may be voices in the wilderness, as more and more marketing brochures arrive in the mail each year, as the pressures of consumerism and fast fashion intensify, and as architects proliferate while projects and clients do not.

11

Architects' Clients

For whom do architects work? Most architectural firms are employed by clients who are contemplating building something. Some architects think of clients only as sources of work and income, but most good architecture is in fact the result of a successful design collaboration between an enlightened architect and an enlightened client. Thus an understanding of clients helps understand architects.

A client may be an individual person, a couple (married or otherwise), or a group of people acting as, or on behalf of, an organization. Legally constituted partnerships and corporations, governments, and agencies of governments can be clients. A lawyer would tell you that, in order to be a legitimate client, an entity needs two things: first, lawful existence as an entity with authority to enter into enforceable contracts; second, money. For architects the latter criterion may pose more problems than the former, since there are loads of clients with no funds, many clients with inadequate funds, some clients with barely enough funds, and almost no clients with unlimited funds.

Architects have great clients and difficult clients. Great clients are perceived to be sympathetic to most, if not all of the architect's design ideas, to give the architect ample design latitude, and to spend money when appropriate, in the interest of artistic patronage. They are decisive, yet accommodating, and never make changes to designs once approved. Such clients also willingly pay the architect's fees and continually praise the architect's work.

Difficult clients obviously display the opposite characteristics. They question the architect's ideas and comprehension of their true programmatic, financial, and scheduling problems. They nitpick, complain about costs, and make decisions slowly. Agonizing forever over each design issue, they often insist that the architect generate limitless design alternatives before agreeing to one. Even then, such clients, according to architects, think nothing of making further changes without consulting the architect. Or they disregard entirely the architect's opinion. And of course many balk when they receive the architect's bill, wondering how a few sheets of drawings could cost so many thousands of dollars.

Great clients respect the architect as a professional, as an artist, and as a problem solver, and they can accept inevitable minor imperfections as part of the price of attaining lofty, aesthetic goals. On the other hand, difficult clients may think of the architect as a necessary but obstructive provider of costly services, insensitive to practical or economic issues, careless, egotistical, and periodically incompetent. Because many clients may have only one direct encounter with an architect during their lifetime, that unique experience may forever color their perception of what architects are like, making them either skeptics or believers.

The Household Client

Let's look at the most plentiful type of client, clients who are demographically households and who seek to enhance the quality of their personal living environments, their homes. "Household" clients, whether singles, couples, families, or communes, hire architects to design a new residence (house or apartment) or to remodel an existing residence. In all cases they need more or better space, shelter, privacy, security, convenience and comfort, and, in some cases, ego satisfaction. The architect is expected to provide a design that can be built by a contractor within the client's budget and that yields a structurally sound, useful, dry, temperate, and easily maintained environment. But the architect and client may strive for more: they may aspire to creating a work of art.

The household client often asks the architect to design not only the building but also the interior environment—furniture, floor coverings, wall and ceiling finishes, decorative trim, colors and fabrics, lighting, window treatments (drapes, shades, blinds), potted plants, artwork, and even ashtrays. But the line between architecture and interior decoration can blur in household design work, since domestic interiors are claimed as the province of another profession, interior designers and decorators.

Intervention by the client, or by decorators, in designing interiors is seen by many architects as unwanted intervention. But all decorators, and many clients, hold the opposite view, insisting that the architecture is mostly the exterior of buildings and, at best, no more than the layout and shaping of interior spaces. From there on, they frequently want their own will, not the architect's, to prevail. As a result many well-conceived works of architecture have been spoiled by bad decorating decisions. Likewise good interior design can help cover up bad architecture.

Household clients can be the most demanding of all client types. Their project may be among the most important single undertakings of their adult lives, financially and psychologically, whether a back porch addition or a new million-dollar home. Residences are personal and intimate places where ego investment can be enormous. Unique behavior occurs there. In our homes we sleep, eat, practice hygiene, make love, read, work, recreate, communicate, socialize, or simply survey that tiny part of the world over which we have dominion.

Home represents an investment not only of money but also of self. So for the household client life's most fundamental needs, desires, activities, experiences and resources are involved. This is why people are willing to commit so much of their lifetime

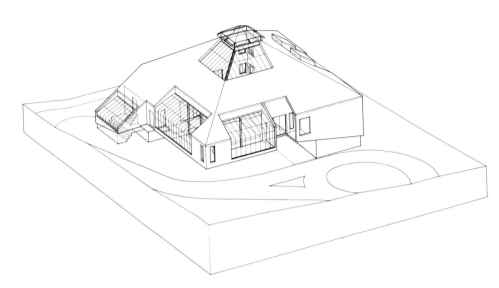

Axonometric view of a unique house for a unique household client (drawing by John Hill).

income (often one-fourth to one-third) and energy to their personal dwelling environment. It is therefore not surprising that household clients can be intensely involved, demanding and emotionally exposed when their home is at stake.

Many clients want fur but can afford cloth. Wanting gourmet quality, they can only pay for takeout. They also expect flawless judgment from the architect, along with speedy design, ability to predict the future, and error-free design and construction. Some clients assume that architects have unlimited control of contractors and unlimited knowledge of building products, not to mention the power to ensure that construction is finished on time and without cost overruns.

For their part architects often expect household clients to be receptive to their every design whim and proposal, to tolerate patiently delays and errors, and to be willing to increase their construction budget in the event that bids come in too high. Architects can fail to warn clients adequately about the limits of the art and science of architecture and construction. The imperfections and unforeseens that may in fact be acceptable to the owners of airports, office buildings, shopping centers, or schools are frequently unacceptable to homeowners.

There is much more than a business relationship established between architects and household clients. To some extent the designer must psychoanalyze the client, becoming familiar with the client's personal habits, tastes, behavior, compulsions, and feelings. The designer may even become enmeshed in the client's domestic affairs, since creating a new home can bring out repressed or unrecognized conflicts and animosities that might not otherwise be revealed. Few architects have not witnessed hostile exchanges between a husband and wife over some design issue, whereupon the architect is suddenly thrust into the role of family counselor and peacemaker. Usually the architect can mediate successfully, but sometimes building a dreamhouse can undo a marriage.

Architects design houses mostly for fun, not for profit. Except for a few plum commissions, most architects are happy just to break even when working for household clients, the majority of whom cannot afford to pay the fees really required to cover all the time and overhead costs. Most large architectural firms won't do houses at all unless they owe a favor to someone. Yet house design continues to receive substantial attention in the media, and from many architects, because designing houses for household clients can permit more opportunity for formal invention. As loss leaders, residential projects may bring bigger, more profitable work in the future due to appreciative household clients of the past.

Developers

Architects would like to believe that their goals are the same as their clients' goals; they frequently are not. In particular, the need or desire for aesthetic self-expression may be secondary to the client, or even nonexistent. This is often true with other than household clients. In the realm of commercial building, of profit-motivated real estate development, clients' motives are quite different from those of clients building homes for themselves. The market-oriented client is primarily interested in one thing: economic success, measured by profit.

The majority of investment in building construction in the United States is commercial development undertaken by private business entities. It includes office buildings, multifamily housing, subdivision housing, retail shopping facilities, industrial and warehouse buildings, and recreational facilities. Clients developing commercial properties view them not so much as works of architecture but rather as investments that produce income, money machines that yield a return on capital. Without the prospect of profit, either directly or through tax benefits, such projects would never be built.

Thus a client whose business is developing commercial property naturally tends toward buildings that cost the least to construct and operate while simultaneously offering the greatest possibility for producing revenue. Here occurs the potential conflict between architect and client, for often the architect proposes designs that achieve the opposite, costing more to construct and operate without corresponding increase in potential revenue and hence less potential investment profit. If construction and operating costs are too high, and revenues too low, actual cash losses will ensue.

Even developers face self-conflict within their own self-defined economic constraints. They must select the level of design quality and amenity necessary to capture the market targeted or to generate anticipated revenues. Otherwise, they risk offering too little for the price and losing the market to competitors who seem to offer more. So the architect tries to sell good design to developer clients on the basis of sound business and investment thinking, arguing that better quality design and increased spending will result in faster and higher rentals or sales. This is a language many commercial clients can understand, although they must be convinced.

To developer clients the ideal architect would thoroughly understand their goals, would know building economics, would always meet budgets and deadlines, would easily obtain approvals from building officials and government review agencies, would turn out error-free, easy-to-read drawings for easy-to-build buildings, and would design buildings that work well and look good at the same time.

There is no shortage of architectural firms who claim to offer all of these things, and certainly some who can deliver. Developers learn quickly about architects and the kinds of services they provide. When they find an architect responsive to their aspirations and requirements, that is the architect they will choose and stick with. As long as this mutuality exists, that architect will have a loyal client. But let something go wrong, and the client may look elsewhere. Naturally there are many architects who may be excellent designers but whom developers would be reluctant to hire.

To many architects the behavior and objectives of real estate developers may seem crass and shortsighted. Architects argue that too many developers sacrifice human or cultural ideals to the so-called "bottom line," rejecting any attempts by architects to design artfully. Developers, say many architects, fail to provide enough time and money to execute projects properly. They feel that some developers are abusive, demanding acquiescence, get-it-done-yesterday performance, and flawless work, all for discounted fees. Architects protest that developer clients commonly use the architect as a banking source by insisting that compensation for services be deferred. In effect the architect's extending credit, which can be for many thousands or tens of thousands of dollars, becomes a condition for getting the design contract.

Some developers and architects believe that art and commerce can be successfully reconciled, although not always easily; it is more difficult to create award-winning architecture in the face of severe economic constraints than when such constraints are relaxed. Although the landscape is littered with thousands of bottom-line buildings which barely qualify as architecture, there are nevertheless many structures that have succeeded both commercially and aesthetically. Regrettably there are also a few that succeeded as architecture but not as investments.

Architects themselves have contributed to sacrificing ideals by sometimes doing mediocre work or by abandoning this sector of the design market to lesser talent. Many developers support this contention by pointing to deficiencies they attribute regularly to architects: delays, cost overruns, unbuildable construction details, wasted space in buildings, overly complex building designs, confusing or incomplete drawings and specifications, incorrect use of materials, poorly coordinated structural or mechanical systems. Although developers are normally more sophisticated about construction, their expectations can equal those of household clients.

An astute developer client would probably assert that creating buildings is a business, not an art, and that their tactics are just sound economic practice. If architects can participate in this business artfully, that's fine, so long as their priorities don't supersede the client's. Some architects are willing to work on these terms, others are not. With each client and project, architects must examine the prospective client's values and compare them with their own. The architect looking for aesthetic patronage will usually not find happiness on the bottom line.

The Corporate Developer

The corporate developer is not just a developer who operates under a corporate umbrella. Rather, the developer, or development team, behaves like a corporation. Corporations of this sort are departmentalized institutions with decision-making responsibility both concentrated at the top and dispersed in the middle. They have several levels of management under the direction of officers who answer to directors who answer to stockholders. Specialization abounds: marketing, finance, production, construction, estimating, purchasing, accounting, project management, property acquisition, and maintenance, to name a few. Each person in the corporation has an interest in what the architect does, but colored by his or her respective area of responsibility.

When the architect designs for a corporate developer, there are really dozens of clients. Marketing managers, concerned with selling or leasing, see the design as a product to be marketed. Construction managers see it as an assemblage of materials and labor. Finance managers and accountants see projects as capital investments, budgets, statements of profit and loss. Property managers see buildings as machines to be maintained after others have built and marketed them. Then there are those overseeing all, the corporation's chief executive officers and active directors. Their interest is corporate concepts, earnings, payable dividends, increased stock value, and corporate image.

Corporate kingdoms may contain multiple territories jealously guarded by their respective territorial overlords, some of whom are subject to delusions of grandeur. Such executives are often both assertive and insecure. They want to succeed in corporate life, to aggrandize their authority and status, to perform well, if not better than their in-house competitors. Corporate managers want to look good within the company along with doing their job properly for the benefit of the company's customers and stockholders.

Architects have to cope with numerous company executives and company politics when working for corporate clients, deciphering the power structure to figure out who makes the ultimate decisions. Once understood, dealing with corporations can become a game which the architect can play and master by letting each individual in the corporate hierarchy believe that his or her opinion is indispensable, that his or her needs are paramount, while still seeking the trust and consent of the top brass.

Many corporate clients are clearheaded, unemotional, and methodical in stating and pursuing their goals, operating in an orderly, well-documented fashion compared to other types of clients. They tend to honor contractual arrangements more willingly, including payment of architects' invoices, partly because institutional, rather than personal funds are involved. But corporations may also prefer to do business with other corporations.

Therefore architectural firms with corporate qualities may appeal to corporate clients, as if corporations had lives and egos of their own, wishing to engage in intimate corporate relations with other corporate entities.

Entrepreneurs

The most frequently encountered commercial client is the individual entrepreneur, the developer whose team is small and who may be building only one or two projects at any given time. He or she may operate using a corporate form of organization or a limited partnership, but the mode of operation clearly bears the caché of one person and one will, unlike most corporate clients.

Entrepreneur clients are closest to being the architect's counterpart. Their egos may be at stake, as well as their fortune (if they have one). They are usually willful, decisive, and outgoing, investing much of themselves in their real estate ventures. They exhibit a certain toughness and resilience, plus the ability to make decisions based on gut instinct rather than intellectual analysis. Some have a sense of mission as well as a desire for wealth. To others development is nothing more than a business in which sizable fortunes can be made or lost with the investment of small amounts of equity and large amounts of borrowed capital.

Historically the entrepreneurs of civilization—political, military, artistic, scientific, and religious figures—sponsored the building of great monuments or cities. The spirit, power, and will of such individual figures resulted in work for architects and builders who would have had little to do without the impetus provided by kings, queens, princes, emperors, moguls, popes, generals, and statesmen of the past. Although the primary goals of these historic entrepreneurs were not related to financial investment opportunities, I suspect that their instincts and compulsions were similar to those of today's developers.

The Institutional Client

The term "institutional" can mean many things to many people and to different architects. However, in architectural practice it usually refers to clients and projects other than those that are primarily investment and profit oriented. Thus this definition usually excludes commercial development. Further institutional clients are generally organizations, corporate or otherwise, that develop projects for very specific purposes. Typical of such projects are the following:

Civic projects—city halls, libraries, concert halls, theaters, and museums.

Schools—elementary and secondary schools, nursery schools, college and university buildings.

Churches, synagogues, and other religious facilities.

Health care facilities—hospitals, nursing homes, clinics.

Institutional headquarters and administrative facilities.

Recreational facilities.

Although a few of the projects may be built for profit-making reasons (such as hospitals and nursing homes), most are not investment real estate.

Institutional clients are much like corporate developers in their organizational characteristics, not surprising for institutions which may in fact be legally constituted corporations. The institution itself may be comprised of a very large constituency, but like corporations with countless stockholders, the institution's behavior is really fashioned by a relatively small number of people who are responsible for making policy and managing the institution's daily affairs.

The architect is almost always faced with a building committee of some sort, delegated by institutional officers, directors, or trustees, some of whom may also be members of the building committee. Other VIPs or experts may also be on the committee, either from within the institution or from outside. Such outside guests may be invited to participate because of their financial resources. Active or potential institutional contributors are obvious favorites for such memberships. In addition project users may be represented on the committee.

Building committees may have substantial decision-making authority, or they may serve in a primarily advisory capacity to another final decision maker (a chief executive officer, or a board of trustees or director). In some cases architects may have to deal with a building committee supplemented by other ad hoc, specialized subcommittees that focus only on specific programmatic and design issues. In these circumstances architects must navigate their course more carefully, since multiple committees can easily be in dispute with one another. Good communication and documentation become essential, not to mention diplomacy.

Institutional clients may be very sophisticated, but many are not experienced in dealing with architectural design and construction. In this regard they can resemble household clients, necessitating efforts by the architect to educate and illuminate. Frequently, when involved with complex projects, institutional clients hire construction management consultants. Construction managers represent the owner's interest in dealing with architects, engineers, general contractors, and subcontractors. They assist in project scheduling, administration and accounting, purchasing, building trade coordination, and cost estimating, acting as a go-between and surrogate client. They can greatly facilitate the process of building when relatively naive institutional clients are involved, but they can also impede it if they duplicate tasks normally carried out by competent architects and contractors.

Some institutional projects have stringent budgets, whereas others may be generously funded. Some are funded privately, through fund-raising campaigns and membership dues, and some receive direct public support and governmental allocations for construction. Aesthetically there are many institutional projects, such as cultural facilities or corporate headquarters, where *image* is important. Here the institutional client must usually provide a budget adequate for such image making by the architect. High budget, high prestige projects—museums, institutional headquarters, civic buildings—tend to lead institutional clients to select architects perceived as having comparable attributes.

Architects like to do projects for institutional clients because in their view there is a much greater chance for producing memorable, newsworthy architecture. Moreover the number of people participating in the development of such projects inevitably increases the architect's contacts and professional exposure. And the special experience of doing special projects may well lead to new project commissions of even greater prestige and expressive potential.

As to fees, institutional clients are more likely to pay their bills than many other kinds of clients, although not necessarily on

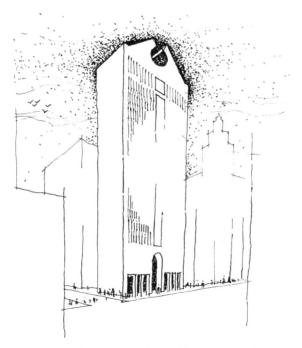

A prestige project by a prestige architect for a prestige client: AT&T's New York headquarters designed by Johnson/Burgee.

time. Architects might also complain about the complexities of coping with a client who acts like a giant committee, who decides things slowly and quasi democratically, and who can be at odds with itself. Design can take longer because the architect must satisfy simultaneously every single person representing the institution's interest. This is even more difficult when personal interests, tastes, and ideologies creep into deliberations. In these circumstances charisma, charm, persistence, and patience become the architect's most valuable assets.

The Government Client

Government clients are a subset of institutional clients. But government agencies and officials have sufficiently interesting characteristics to merit special consideration. Three levels of government predominate: local (municipal or county), state, and federal. Each is composed of executive, legislative, and judicial branches. However, most projects are undertaken by specific *agencies* of government charged with specific missions, typically under the executive branch. Therefore we need to understand how government agencies behave.

Government agencies at all levels build transportation facilities, park and recreation facilities, administrative offices, courts and law enforcement facilities, public hospitals, and housing for low- and moderate-income families. Public educational facilities are built by local and state education agencies. Unique to the federal government are projects for the military, both domestic and overseas, and embassies in foreign countries.

Appropriately governments have created agencies whose concerns lie in these areas. Thus we have departments of transportation, housing and urban development, education, parks, recreation, health, general (administrative) services, and, at the federal level, defense and state. Although funding for construction originates with the legislative budgeting process and is officially carried out under the leadership of the executive, these agencies really provide the impetus and management for conceptualizing and implementing most projects. And of course agencies are themselves corporatelike bodies populated by individual human beings.

Remember that government's objectives are more complicated than industry's. Private enterprise's goal is simple to articulate—profit. The achieving of the goal is easy to imagine—produce and sell a product, a clear and simple statement of mission. Government, however, must protect and further public health, safety, and welfare. It must promote commerce and trade, tax its citizens, provide currency, and undertake any other tasks that need doing but that private enterprise elects not to do. Clearly this is a far more complicated mission to accomplish, for though the ends may seem apparent and indisputable, the means are not.

Looking then at the government agency as a client, the architect will see a collection of people, laws, and regulations, the purpose of which is supposed to be the achievement of public objectives. Moreover such objectives are usually to be achieved at minimum cost to the taxpayer. So most projects built by government are not supposed to be luxurious, flamboyant, or precedent setting. Although there are a few notable and monumental exceptions, most government agencies seek functional, efficient, conservative, proven design whenever they undertake construction.

What are the advantages of working for a governmental client? They are much like those of other institutional and corporate developer clients. First, projects may be large in scope and, as pointed out, of monumental proportions on occasion. Large or small, they can have interesting, challenging programs. Second, government-sponsored projects ordinarily serve some public purpose which may prove to be a source of satisfaction to those contributing to it. Third, the successful completion of one government commission may well lead to another in the same area of specialization. Fourth, once a contract for services is negotiated and signed, government agencies reliably pay fees earned for services rendered, unless there are disputes. Fifth, most governmental clients provide the architect with a clearly stated budget and list of requirements, though not always.

On the opposite side of the ledger reside some serious disadvantages of which architects must be aware. They are in effect a mirror image of the advantages. Projects can be banal, mundane, and architecturally unpromising, no matter how talented the architect or well-intentioned the government sponsor. Fees can be ridiculously tight or inadequate, sometimes even limited by statute despite the amount of work required of the architect. Negotiating acceptable contracts with government agencies can be excruciating, particularly when officials can always argue that somewhere out there is a firm willing to do the project for a lower fee. And, if a dispute arises later, many government agencies think nothing of holding the architect's feet to the fire by withholding fee payment, knowing that the architect has little recourse.

Perhaps the worst attribute associated with the government client is the so-called bureaucratic mentality. Not all government officials have it. In fact it is a characteristic not limited to government agencies. Such minds can be found in private corporations, institutions, and architects' offices. But the word "bureaucrat" has become most closely associated with government. What characterizes bureaucrats, negatively speaking? Above all it is their attitude, not their competence or expertise, although these too may be in question at times. This attitude is best described as a "can't do," "no way" approach.

The negative bureaucrat, in contrast to the positive bureaucrat, looks for reasons *not* to do or approve things. He or she plays as literally as possible by the book and the regulations, and when in doubt, says no. Such persons tend to be dogmatic and inflexible. They abhor uncertainty, which is of course the realm in which architects dwell. They shun taking risks and responsibility for any actions that are not clearly prescribed for them in writing. Since no code or regulation can ever anticipate every eventuality, negative bureaucrats can be major obstacles in the path of creative architects.

Equally regrettable are those bureaucrats who almost instinctively resist innovation, change, or experimentation, despite the potential for improvement or discovery. Many are motivated by basic job security concerns. They fear criticism and will do almost anything to cover their respective posteriors. Even more discouraging, and enfuriating as well, are bureaucrats who exhibit suspicion and skepticism concerning the motives of people with whom their agency interacts. Acting ostensibly to protect the public interest and save taxpayers' money, such officials often assume that private interests are up to something—cutting corners, charging exorbitant fees, padding expenses, conspiring with other consultants or contractors. Also, like some other types of clients, they may expect an unattainable level of perfection.

Agencies themselves, being bureaucracies, can behave this way collectively. Sometimes the architect finds that negativism is the dominant policy, particularly regarding creativity in design. For example, many school boards and departments of education have adopted regulations and specifications that permit only the most conventional of design solutions for school buildings. The U.S. Army Corps of Engineers is notorious for its strictly "engineering" approach to building design, an approach it demands from the architects it hires. For many years the Federal Housing Authority (FHA) promulgated design standards and other regulations that made it extremely difficult for architects to develop innovative housing projects, even to save money.

Architects experience frustration in still other ways when working for governments. Changes in personnel can deter the progress of a project's design, since new contracting officials may have quite different views or interpretations of mandates than their predecessors. This can occur most dramatically with changes of administration following elections. Sometimes the project itself may be suspended or terminated. Budgets and building requirements may be altered suddenly, compelling the architect to modify or recommence the design.

Once designed, most projects built by government agencies are competitively bid, since this theoretically ensures that the public will obtain the best price possible in the construction marketplace. Unfortunately it also means that neither the agency nor the architect knows what the project will actually cost until most of the architectural work is completed. If the budget and interim estimates have been unrealistically low, bidding results can come as a great shock to all. In some cases government agencies insist on revisions by the architect without additional compensation, or they abandon the architect's plans altogether. At best this is an embarrassment to the architect and may make collecting all of the fees earned difficult. Unfortunately this can occur with nongovernmental clients as well.

There are many architectural firms that have never done a government project, whereas others specialize in them. Some firms thrive collaborating with government agencies, but some, having tried it once or twice, have given up, claiming they only lost money and gained ulcers. In all cases the type of client you will have depends on the type of architect you become.

12

Architects as Types

The preface to this book refers to several popular versions of architects in action, of architects as heroes in one form or another. The image of the architect, for most readers not yet architects or architects' clients, is probably highly romanticized. Unfortunately such images are prone to be erroneous and vastly oversimplified, since most architects are complex, amalgamated personalities. Therefore my intention in this final chapter is to describe what many architects are really like.

My strategy is to list "types" by citing dominant, observable patterns of behavior, personal style, and aptitude. No single type can adequately represent any single architect or person. Therefore the reader must "mix and match" these variously described characteristics to obtain a complete description of a particular architect, or of themselves. Although one type may predominate, most architects are a combination of types, just as one might expect in a profession where the mix of egos and disciplines is so rich. Remember that you may obtain an insightful glimpse of the type of architect you are or might become.

The Highborn

It's been said that some people were born to be architects, possessing some rare set of talents ideally suited to the field. Others are born into circumstances that facilitate their achieving personal and professional goals with minimal resistance. These are "highborn" individuals who, in addition to their intellectual and artistic talents, are blessed with access to already accumulated wealth, social standing, and savoir faire.

The highborn type, for whom economic and social status is natural and normal, may have entrée to a world of potential clients not available to many others. Comfortable and confident, many of them can practice architecture without being obliged to make a living at it. They can afford to approach architecture more as an artistic and cultural diversion than as a business or career.

Being highborn is obviously an advantage for a prospective architect. If one is liberated from the fetters of subsistence economics, then more selective exploration and ego indulgence are possible. If one has grown up among the elite, if one feels at home in the salons of affluence, and if the elite do indeed influence much of what is built, then being an elite architect can often be a sure ticket to success. Nevertheless, some amount of talent and skill is still required, along with hard work, to be a successful architect. Just being highborn will usually not suffice.

The Artiste

The "artiste" in architecture is defined by manner and outlook. The dictionary says that an artiste is "a skilled adept performer," an "entertainer." Artistes communicate artistic concern and commitment through gestures and words. Sometimes they are totally preoccupied with being what they are and expressing themselves flamboyantly and unconventionally. None of this reflects necessarily on the artiste architect's inherent talent or intellect, which may be exceptional.

Artistes can be humorous, witty, deadly serious, ironic, manic-depressive, or dramatic, but never shy or reticent. They are demonstrative and relish an audience. Much of what artistes do will be consciously chosen or fashioned to express their artistry and taste, to put on a show: what they wear, how they live, the authors they read and quote, the diversions they seek. They tend always to strike a pose, no matter what they are doing. They may or may not be outstanding architects.

The Prima Donna

Common to all professions, but perhaps extreme in architecture, are the "prima donna" types. They are found in academe and in architectural offices. They seem oblivious to and even disdainful toward other people, others ideas, and other activities unconnected to their immediate interests and needs. Their comportment is sometimes one of arrogance and hauteur. They often seem vain and temperamental, at times unapproachable. In some cases they are capable of unforgettable exhibitions of pomposity.

Prima donnas may well be artistes too, affecting flamboyant or even rebellious nonconformity, shunning that which they consider mundane or banal. Some prima donnas have risen to the part naturally, having established themselves without question as authoritative, brilliant, or extraordinary figures. Other prima donnas are less deserving of such self-generated status. Only their self-estimation, not the estimation of others, has placed them on a pedestal. Humility seems to elude many prima donna architects who won't hesitate to tell you how great they are.

The Intellectual

Most educated folk think of themselves as intellectually capable. The "intellectual," on the other hand, is not merely someone who is well educated but is rather someone primarily interested in the cultivation and analysis of ideas, concepts, history, and theory, all properly footnoted.

In architecture the intellectual designer is concerned with more than making things look and perform well. He or she is concerned with the cultural, literary, and poetic content of architecture, arrived at through rigorous thought and research. He or she likes words as well as buildings—sometimes the bigger the words, the better. Esoteric reasoning and little-known facts deepen the significance of truly intellectual work.

Intellectuals can become impatient with those whose thinking or approach lacks intellectual merit or profundity. Like prima donnas intellectuals may appear to be snobbish or aloof. Anti-intellectuals accuse them of producing or thriving on an excess of obtuse, obscure, contrived, or irrelevant matter. But the honest, unpretentious intellectual provides analysis and stimulation essential to the creation and preservation of our architectural heritage.

The Critic

Cousin to the intellectual is the "critic." Critics are usually authentic or would-be intellectuals who pronounce judgment on the work of others, regardless of whether they themselves can produce such work. The critic type abounds in architecture, since criticism is the fundamental method by which architecture is taught and evaluated. The critic architect may or may not design good buildings. He or she may not even practice architecture.

After assessing the quality of others' work, critics are usually eager to share their assessment with anyone who is interested in listening. They too need an audience. They must also be fairly articulate, both in writing and speaking, in order to impress their audience and get their message across. Good critics, of which there are more needed, are essential in architecture, for they tell us convincingly what we are doing well and not so well, and why. They can guide us and motivate us to do better when their criticism is instructional and insightful.

But much architectural criticism is less than constructive. Poor critics offer criticism that may be sarcastic, inaccurate, ill informed, superficial, narrow-minded, or misleading. Some may be prone to word games, substituting whim and wit for rational, balanced evaluation and clear expression. Occasionally they just talk gibberish. If they have the public's attention through the media, they may become tastemakers, assuming power to promote those they personally favor and demote those they disapprove. They may fall prey to the unreasonable influence of certain architects, fads, movements, or other critics with which they are sympathetic. Passing trends and fashions may unduly sway them. Whether good or bad at what they do, the critic types in architecture always have a definitive opinion of everyone else's work.

The Down-to-Earther

Many architects are of the "down-to-earth" type. Down-to-earthers, as the phrase implies, are practical, get-the-job-done people. They focus on reality, on facts, on tangible and pragmatic results that can be understood and utilized. They may seem to be anti-intellectual. In architecture the down-to-earther is interested in intellectualized concepts only to the extent that they withstand the tests of common sense and practicality. They like building for its own sake and thrive on the nitty-gritty process of creating the built environment. They worry about cost, schedules, and making things workable. Fantasizing, aesthetic speculation, verbal theorizing, and radical experimentation are normally avoided by down-to-earthers. They are less concerned about the meaning of beauty than in finding the means to achieve beauty.

The down-to-earth architect may have substantial technical aptitude. He or she may also have strong management and organizational skills, reflecting the concern with implementation. We speak of architects who really know how to "put buildings together," implying that they are extremely knowledgeable about detailed design, construction materials and systems, and construction procedures. These same architects, by their very nature, tend to resist generating new aesthetic directions in architecture. They refine and resolve more than they invent. But excessive practicality can be an impediment to the development of new thinking and new solutions, since the most practical approach is often to repeat what was done before. So there is a

strong argument for teaming up down-to-earthers with intellectuals and fantasizers, those who create ideas with those who can
execute them.

The Anal-Compulsive

Comes now the "anal-compulsive." "Anal," by dictionary
definition, has come to signify adult traits such as orderliness
and obstinacy. Compulsives are everywhere, with plenty in architecture. Whatever their other characteristics—one could be,
after all, a down-to-earth, intellectual, highborn critic—the anal-
compulsive breed continuously pursues certain things as if obsessed by them. Obsessive personalities are usually viewed
as "uptight," inflexible, demanding, and occasionally self-
righteous. However, we must acknowledge that there are good
obsessions and bad ones. Like the other types presented so far,
the anal-compulsive has a place in architecture.

Thousands of tasks exist in architectural practice that require intense, careful, thorough execution. Details can be everything. As
the reader must now realize, the potential for costly errors is
high. Thus, being compulsive about completing a task one hundred percent can be an asset in an architectural office. Neatness,
with its associated obsessions, can be an asset, along with many
other obsessions. Exhaustive, nit-picking, time-intensive work
must be diligently and meticulously carried out in order to
design and construct good architecture, making compulsive
architects indispensable. Moreover the safety of the public
depends on such diligence; one would feel much more comfortable occupying a building whose design was scrutinized by an
anal-compulsive than by a hang-loose, laid-back casual type.

Like most types, being anal-compulsive can also be a liability.
Taken to an extreme, or misdirected, obsessive behavior can be
very destructive. It can induce mental and emotional blindness,
cutting off whole realms of possibilities for the victim. It can
make one unreasonably stubborn, obstructionist, and biased in
ways not intended. The excessively compulsive architect can

alienate colleagues and clients with his or her refusal to let go, to "get off it." Obsession impedes fruitful negotiation and new discovery, being perceived as arrogant, irrational, and psychotic behavior . . . if it's excessive.

Anal-compulsive architects sometimes perpetrate ghastly architecture when driven by personal obsession with their own bad ideas. They may be stylistically compulsive or compulsive about certain building materials or colors, despite their appropriateness. However, being obsessed should not be confused with thoughtfully taking and defending a position, the latter being crucial for the architect. Indeed, a very fine line separates vigorous advocacy from compulsive defensiveness, but it is an important distinction.

The Plodder

Architectural offices and schools are full of "plodders." Plodders, like down-to-earthers and anal-compulsives, can be effective in architectural practice. They are best characterized as people who exhibit a willingness, if not a desire, to undertake work that requires steady, continuous, laborious, and potentially monotonous effort. They just keep on going, plugging away, until their job is done. They seem to be able to thrive on drudgery, of which there is much in architecture. They can handle repetitive tasks or tasks comprised of many separate steps. They accept routine. The plodder is persistent but not necessarily compulsive. Faced with an obstacle or change of direction, he or she may have no trouble adjusting forward movement to adapt to the changed circumstances. Most plodders are agreeable sorts. They rarely support causes to be fought for, nor do they espouse obscure theories. And they generally respect authority, gladly receiving instruction or guidance when appropriate.

Many people are plodders. Without plodders, our entire society would cease functioning, for most jobs require plodding along. Drafting rooms are full of architectural plodders, usually down-to-earthers as well. They perform drafting, write specifications, conduct research, manage projects, meet with salespeople, sort through catalogs, and do a hundred other pieces of work that make up the day-to-day routine in an architectural firm. Like society as a whole we architects would have difficulty functioning without an adequate supply of plodders.

The Social Worker

I have suggested that the humanitarian instinct is one which can be productively satisfied in architecture. Not surprisingly, many architects can be typed as "social workers." The social worker is concerned with helping people, particularly those who are unable to help themselves. Social worker architects see architecture as a means, rather than as an end, a means to improve public welfare through environmental design intervention. It's a cause that they feel is noble, relevant, and fulfilling. Some advocate their cause with great passion and fervor. They are very user oriented, admonishing those architects who would sacrifice user satisfaction and social responsibility to the demands of personal aesthetic indulgence. It's not that social workers are unconcerned with aesthetics, but their priorities are different than those of architects who are interested primarily in stylistic and intellectual issues.

The social worker in architecture was far more prevalent in the 1960s and 1970s, or at least more frequently heard from. They formed alliances with local communities, joined the Peace Corps and Vista, worked in urban ghettos, and advocated architecture by and for the masses. Being a competent designer was not enough. One had to become politically and diplomatically aware and active. Sociology and psychology had to be added to the architect's already broad collection of expertise.

Social worker architects want the user and the client to become surrogate architects, to design from the bottom up instead of from the top down. After all, they argue, people feel helpless because they have no control over shaping the environment—

housing, neighborhoods, buildings, and cities—that in turn shapes their lives. Certain kinds of architectural projects appeal most to the social worker type: housing for the elderly and handicapped, low-income housing, schools, health and recreational facilities, and prisons. These increase the opportunity to get involved with needy users, to be charitable, and affect the greatest number of people.

During two years spent in the Peace Corps, I and my fellow volunteers believed that we were giving testimony to our societal concern, to the notion that architecture had an exalted social purpose. We wanted both to do good and to do good architecture by designing schools and housing instead of exotic villas for wealthy patrons. But most architects, including many social worker types, eventually discover that the extent of enduring social reform and welfare attainable through architecture is surprisingly limited, and they soon learn that to survive, they must adopt a "Robin Hood" approach.

The Fantasizer

We all indulge in fantasies from time to time, although some of us fantasize regularly. Architecture has always had its share of "fantasizers," architects who continually dream up and propose buildings that seem impossible or unrealizable. The opposite of the down-to-earther, the fantasizer is not hamstrung or deterred by matters of practicality, convention, or acceptability. He or she is a speculator and a risk taker in the territory of ideas. Architectural fantasizers may have a keen sense of history, since much of today's reality was yesterday's fantasy. The fantasizer may also take pleasure in being outrageous and iconoclastic, using expressions of fantasy as a form of criticism or commentary. Proposals of fantasy can be satirical, vexatious, and enlightening all at the same time. Most fantasizers are very creative, whatever their motivations.

Fantasizers do not necessarily attempt to forecast or determine the future course of architecture. Often they brew up fantasy for

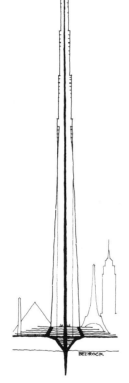

Frank Lloyd Wright's proposed mile high tower for Chicago,
the "Illinois," to contain 18,462,000 square feet of space and
130,000 occupants.

its own sake, to be whimsical and amusing. Architectural fantasy can relate to style, technology, ornamentation, or symbolism. It can also be economic pie in the sky, since much of the fantasy dreamed up by architects is either undoable or unaffordable. A look at the pyramids of Egypt again suggests that they were someone's fantasy before they were built. And they were certainly not intended to establish a new direction for Egyptian or any other architecture.

Architectural fantasy can be provocative, challenging, and foretelling, occasionally resulting in real-world monuments or breakthroughs. Only when fantasizers offer fantasy masquerading as reality, or fantasy that conceals or denies reality, do their efforts meet with skepticism and disapproval. Fantasy is perhaps riskiest when used to escape reality. For prospective architects and architectural students the danger posed by fantasy is that it may be confused with reality.

The Manager

Let us now jump abruptly from the realm of fantasy to the realm of business. There is a group of architect types that fall under the heading of business types. Some are "managers," some are "entrepreneurs," some are "hustlers," and some are "joiners." They are related but distinguishable types, and we will consider them separately.

The manager likes to run things. Managers thrive on administration, whether or not they are adept at it. They like to be in charge, to have power, to direct people and conduct operations. They enjoy shouldering responsibility and exercising authority. If they are effective, they generally have leadership ability, the ability to make decisions in situations of conflict and pressure. Their instincts draw them to organizations and to organizational politics.

Structured management is required in architectural practice, both to manage projects and firms. In this respect architecture is like any business. Firm accounts, finances, personnel, business development, and physical facilities have to be administered, along with the specific operations occurring for each project within the firm. Without manager types, who may do much more than manage, organizational chaos and economic disaster would be likely.

Today management has become a field of specialization, a twentieth-century accredited discipline. Professional managers are among the most highly paid workers, since the effectiveness of management can significantly influence the fate of any business. But managers who are too anal-compulsive can be a problem. Management for its own sake can take over. The purpose of management and managers is to plan and operate some system of activity by supporting the personnel carrying out the activity, all of which is intended to achieve the system's goals, whatever they may be. Management's purpose is not merely to proliferate itself. Managers obsessed with administrative structure or infatuated by organizational protocols and techniques can lose sight of their goals and stifle those working under them.

The laissez-faire manager can be just as obstructive, but in a much more passive way. These manager types, not being compulsive about controlling or monitoring all activities in detail, tend to let people operate independently at their own pace. They intervene only when forced to. Here the risk is in letting things slip out of control, or slip by altogether. Although the casual manager may superficially maintain smoother, more amiable relations with the people he or she is overseeing, the lack of attention or direction may result in inefficiency, financial loss, frustration on the part of underlings, and even failure in the mission.

The ideal manager is a mix of these two subtypes. Of course he or she can also have characteristics of many other of the types already described. Good managers may not always be loved, but they will be respected, listened to, followed, and usually rewarded, no matter how obnoxiously or sweetly they may behave from time to time.

The Entrepreneur

The "entrepreneur" type and the manager are not automatically interchangeable. Entrepreneurs are characterized by several unique qualities. They are, first and above all, risk takers, especially financial risk. They are willing to accept the possibility of losses as well as profits. And they enjoy taking risks, either consciously or subconsciously. A manager is not necessarily motivated by the thrill of taking risks.

Second, the entrepreneur type likes to create and control his or her business or project, to own it, not just manage it. They are initiators and implementers of their own ideas. Third, the entrepreneur is very market conscious, always alert to project opportunities that might arise. Unmet needs, new areas of growth, or unprecedented product or design concepts are what they seek. Finding them, they try to exploit them. Their aim is to foster new activity and interest where there was none before.

Entrepreneur types are not all developers of real estate or founders of architectural firms. Anyone who enjoys generating ideas and then mustering resources to implement them is an entrepreneur. One may not own the product produced (in the sense of having title to it), but its ownership may be felt by way of authorship and the satisfaction of figurative parenthood.

The Hustler

Many entrepreneurs are also "hustlers," some because they have to be, others because they truly enjoy hustling. The term is slightly pejorative. The hustler may be a pushy, zealous, ambitious type who expends much time and energy chasing opportunity and people. Of course good salespeople have to hustle, looking for openings, following up leads. Social skills go with hustling, for hustlers must flatter, curry favor, ingratiate, and persuade. Effective hustlers are extroverts, exuding confidence and volunteering advice when needed. They must be reasonably sensitive to what others are looking for, as all selling represents an exchange between mutually consenting parties.

Effective hustlers are not automatically effective entrepreneurs or managers. In business those who sell may not be those who oversee operations. As architectural practice requires selling services, it is not surprising that some architects are willing and able to hustle and to do it well. But others are put off by the prospect of hustling with its negative connotations of pretense, hypocrisy, and misrepresentation.

Some people believe that the hustler is obliged to exaggerate and, like politicians, make promises known to be appetizing but unrealistic. The hustler is presumed to be putting on an act, saying and doing things which he or she may not really believe in or care to do, buttering up people for business or social purposes when such people might not otherwise be of interest. Hustling is condemned because it smacks of commerce and trade instead of quiet, deliberative professionalism. But hustlers can also work subtly, and they can be highborn and intellectual, artistes or down-to-earthers. Whether acknowledged or not, architects are all obliged to hustle from time to time.

The Joiner

Perhaps the "joiner" is a special form of hustler. Joiners affiliate. They belong to organizations and associations in which they can participate, be seen and heard, and mix with both colleagues and prospective clients. Their outgoing, associative nature allows them to meet lots of people, exchange ideas, gather information and project leads, and make themselves or their firms more widely known. Joining, as the word itself suggests, is a popular method for conducting public relations.

Joiners have a vast array of groups to choose from. There are local, state, national, and international organizations of all types. Many are professional, comprised primarily of architects, such as the AIA. Others are business organizations such as chambers-of-commerce or rotary clubs. Local civic and community organizations are plentiful. Some of these are related to culture and the arts, some to education, some to the environment, and some to political causes. Architects often find their way onto local governing boards, giving them the opportunity not only to belong but also to influence public policy.

One encounters many architects who have joined clubs. There are country clubs, social clubs, men's clubs, women's clubs, alumni and university clubs, dinner clubs, racquet clubs, and clubs organized for a thousand other reasons. Club joiners may not only have a good time, they may also directly or indirectly generate new business doing it.

The Poet-Philosopher

Departing from the realm of business, let us return to the more mysterious realm of philosophers. Every period, movement, and trend in architecture produces architects or is produced by architects who are seen as "poet-philosophers," transmitters of messages transcending the literal, objective content of architectural form. Poet-philosophers are found in both practice and academe, often implementing in the former what they preach in the latter.

Poet-philosophers, who may also be artistes, intellectuals, fantasizers, or entrepreneurs, usually subscribe to theories and rationales that offer more than "commodity, firmness, and delight." To them architecture's essence resides in its literary, cultural, symbolic, and philosophical significance. They may see their role as interpreting and answering cosmic questions regarding humanity's search for historical identity, dignity, spiritual enrichment and comprehension, or justice. They are not content with just designing and constructing beautiful buildings that are useful and attractive. Architecture must have a larger purpose.

The poet-philosopher usually embraces some kind of very personal theory of design, finding linkages to sources in traditional philosophy, religion, literature, history, or the arts, particularly painting, sculpture, and music. Although he or she ultimately tests such theories through conventional graphic and visual means, the conscious development and exposition of them is frequently verbal. Poet-philosophers are compelled to talk and write about their vision of architecture, to explain it in personal terms.

Often the poetic, verbal presentation of such philosophy and accompanying work inspires admirers and followers. Thus poet-philosophers can become veritable "gurus." As such they may equate buildings with poetry, books, or ideologies, asking that we "read" their architecture and interpret it accordingly. If we are unable to do so on our own, they usually stand ready to do it for us, either by writing it down or telling us. Such discourses can be fascinating and wondrous or, at worst, obscure and pedantic. Sometimes it can sound irrelevant or contrived, bearing little relationship to the tangible architecture at hand.

Some poet-philosopher architects maintain a consistent approach, one that the astute observer can perceive in their work and that clearly infuses the work throughout its creation and realization over time. However, there are others who make observers suspicious of the genuineness of such philosophizing because what is read or said appears to have been generated after the fact. Suspicious observers may claim that these architects, consciously aspiring to don the mantle of poet-philosopher, are tempted to invent poetic or philosophical rationales that were never present or appropriate when a given work was created.

If buildings really are poems or manifestos, then there is nothing affected or pretentious about this impulse to see them on a higher plane. Much architecture is readable and rich in messages, many of which architects never anticipated. Too often, though, we hear pronouncements of meaning and symbolism that only the architect, along with a select group of sympathetic critics and disciples, can see or interpret—that seem to elude the rest of us no matter how hard we try to make sense of them. In these circumstances the suspicions are justified.

Many famous architects were poet-philosophers. Frank Lloyd
Wright, Le Corbusier, and Louis Kahn, for example, were designers whose verbally stated philosophies and theories could
stimulate as much as their buildings could. Poetry is fashioned
with metaphors, and these and other architects commonly approached buildings as metaphors—of nature, machines, freedom, the human form, abstract geometry, music, heaven, and
the like. Some poet-philosophers, like Paolo Soleri, who is building his vision of an urban utopia in the Arizona desert, have
transformed their concept of architecture into philosophical,
architectural movements or schools of thought. In turn their
adherents act as advocates, and if their design philosophy is
widely accepted, it may eventually become part of mainstream
architecture. Unfortunately lesser minds and hands can distort

Frank Lloyd Wright in his studio.

or misuse such legacies, weakening them in the process. And nothing in architecture is so boring as overworked, tiresome design clichés that are the residue of some poet-philosopher's original ideas.

The Renaissance Person

Let's end this chapter with a description of the type of architect that many strive to be, perhaps the ideal in the view of some: the "Renaissance person" (it used to be "man"). Recall that the Renaissance in Europe is considered the age of secular enlightenment and humanism, that it produced some of civilization's most creative and expansive minds—men like Leonardo de Vinci, Michaelangelo, and Palladio. They were inventors, artists, architects, philosophers, craftsmen, scientists, engineers, and builders. Thus we commonly talk of the Renaissance person as someone of many talents, someone versatile, intelligent, inventive, and skillful, a generalist rather than a specialist.

If you review all of the foregoing types found in architecture and imagine an architect embodying most of them, then you would have conceived of such a person, assuming of course that he or she possessed the basic talents and know-how necessary to be an architect. It is the comprehensive and many-disciplined nature of architecture that engenders the Renaissance mind and spirit. Architects are expected to help orchestrate many processes and people, to possess expertise in a variety of areas, and to apply diverse skills in situations of uncertainty and change. They must be able to work intelligently with masons as well as bankers, with accountants as well as digital computers.

Trying to be a Renaissance person is challenging, but many architects come close to it. They are able to manage and organize their lives and work to do it all, and in great quantity. And, although the prolific Renaissance architect of today may not always produce cutting-edge or timeless architecture, he or she may very well be the type who has the best crack at it.

Afterword

There is much commentary embedded in each of the chapters of this book, but I am compelled to add an optional postscript.

On Becoming an Architect

- After high school students should spend at least two years, if not four, pursuing college-level general education before concentrating on architecture in a professional program—play the field of electives, explore diverse interests, have flings, compete in athletics—prior to total architectural immersion. This is a distinct advantage of graduate programs over five-year undergraduate programs.

- If you are studying architecture, but you're doing poorly or feeling unhappy about it, consider alternatives—taking a year off to work, enrolling in fewer courses, or even changing majors.

- Schools, although not necessarily all schools, should offer more optional tracks for students after completion of basic architectural studies; these tracks would be alternatives to the traditional track emphasizing conceptual design. This seems appropriate, since many architectural students are weak as conceptual designers while having strengths in other areas—detailed design, urban planning, technology, construction, business and management, for example. Because the history, evolution, and postulation of aesthetic ideas are so revered in academe, it has been difficult to generate enthusiasm and support for such options.

• Architectural schools should educate fewer but better architects. At the same time they should seek more institutional support for expanding the nonprofessional components of their programs, allowing them to offer more courses for undergraduates and others not intending to seek professional architectural degrees but who are interested in the subject. However, the concentrated professional programs should have first priority and should not be compromised for the sake of nonprofessional, general education.

On Being an Architect

• If and when you marry, consider its impact on your career, and your career's impact on your marriage; there are many divorced architects!

• Take your time. There's no rush. You don't have to do it all before you're thirty, or even forty. You have much to learn, and architects are students all their lives, always capable of learning new things and starting in new directions at any age.

• Be assured that today's superficial fads and fashions will be stale tomorrow and gone by next week. What seems important now may be inconsequential in the future. Therefore architects must search for more lasting values, just as their buildings may last for many decades or centuries. The same can be said about what architectural journalists, critics, and jurors search for in judging architecture.

• Architects should resist the temptation to be all things to all people. Genuine architects do best when they are doing architecture. Architects are not engineers, contractors, sociologists, financial analysts, or developers. Therefore we should concentrate our efforts on improving the circumstances that relate directly to architecture and architectural practice, avoiding periodic forays into other territory for the sake of economic expedience or professional annexation. Being good at designing physical environments is a great enough challenge.

Finally, it is worth recalling what makes architecture such an appealing profession to so many: the excitement and rewards of creativity through design and building; the transformation of complex programs into useful and visually rich environments; the fusion of art, technology, and the social sciences in one discipline; and the occasional gratitude and recognition bestowed by respectful clients, colleagues, and the public. Despite the impediments, frustrations, financial limitations, and risks that architects must cope with, few careers are as potentially challenging. For those with talent, motivation, and some amount of good luck, no career is quite like architecture.

Appendix: Accredited Programs in Architecture

The Association of Collegiate Schools of Architecture (ACSA), 1735 New York Avenue, N.W., Washington, D.C., 20006, publishes a book entitled *Architecture Schools in North America* that includes comprehensive descriptions of all schools in North America offering accredited architectural programs. Contact schools individually to obtain specific information about programs, degrees, costs, financial aid, faculty, and admissions requirements. In this appendix we reprint the list of programs issued by the National Architectural Accrediting Board, effective 1 January 1983:

Arizona, University of, College of Architecture
Tucson, Arizona 85721
Ronald Gourley, FAIA, Dean   602 621-6751

Arizona State University, College of Architecture
Tempe, Arizona 85287
Roger Schluntz, AIA, Chairman   602 965-3536

Arkansas, University of, School of Architecture
Fayetteville, Arkansas 72701
C. Murray Smart, Jr., AIA, Dean   501 575-4705

Auburn University, Department of Architecture
Auburn, Alabama 36849
R. Wayne Drummond, AIA, Head   205 826-4516

Ball State University, College of Architecture
and Planning, Muncie, Indiana 47306
Robert A. Fisher, AIA, Dean   317 285-4481

Boston Architectural Center, 320 Newbury Street
Boston, Massachusetts 02115
Bernard P. Spring, FAIA, President   617 536-3170

University of California, Berkeley, Department of
Architecture, Berkeley, California 94720
Jean-Pierre Protzen, Acting Chair   415 642-4942

University of California, Los Angeles, Graduate School of
Architecture and Urban Planning
Los Angeles, California 90024
Samuel Aroni, Acting Dean   213 825-4091

California Polytechnic State University, Architecture
Department, School of Architecture and Environmental Design,
San Luis Obispo, California 93407
Don Koberg, Interim Head   805 546-1316

California State Polytechnic University, Pomona
School of Environmental Design,
Department of Architecture, Pomona, California 91768
Patrick Sullivan, AIA, Chair   714 598-4171

Carnegie-Mellon University, Department of Architecture
Pittsburgh, Pennsylvania 15213
Ömer Akin, AIA, Head   412 578-2355

Catholic University of America, Department of
Architecture and Planning, Washington, D.C. 20064
Peter Blake, AIA, Chairman   202 635-5188/89

Cincinnati, University of, School of Architecture and
Interior Design, Cincinnati, Ohio 45221
John Meunier, Director   513 475-6426

City College of the City University of New York
School of Architecture and Environmental Studies
New York, New York 10031
Donald E. Mintz, Acting Dean   212 690-4118

Clemson University, College of Architecture
Clemson, South Carolina 29631
Harlan E. McClure, FAIA, Dean   803 656-3081

Colorado, University of, College of Design and Planning
Denver, Colorado 80202 Boulder, Colorado 80309
John Prosser, AIA, Acting Dean   303 629-2755

Columbia University, Graduate School of
Architecture and Planning
New York, New York 10027
James Stewart Polshek, FAIA, Dean   212 280-3414

Cooper Union, The Irwin S. Chanin School of Architecture
New York, New York 10003
John Hejduk, FAIA, Dean   212 254-6300

Cornell University, Department of Architecture
Ithaca, New York 14853
Jerry A. Wells, AIA, Chairman   607 256-5236

Detroit, University of, School of Architecture
Detroit, Michigan 48221
Bruno Leon, FAIA, Dean   313 927-1149

Drexel University (Evening College), Department of
Architecture, Philadelphia, Pennsylvania 19104
Peter F. Arfaa, FAIA, Head   215 895-2159

Florida, University of, Department of Architecture
Gainesville, Florida 32611
John M. McRae, Chairman   904 392-0205

Florida A & M University, School of Architecture
Tallahassee, Florida 32307
Richard K. Chalmers, AIA, Dean   904 599-3244

Georgia Institute of Technology, College of Architecture
Atlanta, Georgia 30332
William L. Fash, Dean   404 894-3881

Hampton Institute, Department of Architecture
Hampton, Virginia 23668
John H. Spencer, FAIA, Chairman   804 727-5440/41

Harvard University, Department of Architecture
Cambridge, Massachusetts 02138
Henry N. Cobb, FAIA, Chairman   617 495-2591

Hawaii, University of, College of Architecture
Honolulu, Hawaii 96822
Elmer Botsai, FAIA, Dean   808 948-7225

Houston, University of, College of Architecture
Houston, Texas 77004
William R. Jenkins, FAIA, Dean   713 749-1188

Howard University, School of Architecture and
Planning, Washington, D.C. 20059
Harry G. Robinson III, AIA, Dean   202 636-7420

Idaho, University of, College of Art and Architecture,
Moscow, Idaho 83843
Paul L. Blanton, FAIA, Dean   208 885-6272

Illinois Institute of Technology, College of Architecture,
Planning and Design, Chicago, Illinois 60616
George Schipporeit, AIA, Dean   312 567-3262

Illinois at Chicago, University of, School of Architecture
Box 4348, Chicago, Illinois 60680
Thomas H. Beeby, AIA, Director   312 996-3335

Illinois, University of, School of Architecture
608 East Lorado Taft Drive, Champaign, Illinois 61820
R. Alan Forrester, Director   217 333-1330

Iowa State University, Department of Architecture
Ames, Iowa 50011
Kenneth E. Carpenter, AIA, Chairman   515 294-4717

Kansas, University of, School of Architecture and Urban
Design, Lawrence, Kansas 66044
W. Max Lucas, Jr., Dean   913 864-4281

Kansas State University, College of Architecture and
Design, Manhattan, Kansas 66506
Bernd Foerster, FAIA, Dean   913 532-5951

Kent State University, School of Architecture and
Environmental Design, Kent, Ohio 44242
Foster D. Armstrong, AIA, Acting Director   216 672-2917

Kentucky, University of, College of Architecture
Lexington, Kentucky 40506
Anthony Eardley, Dean   606 257-7619

Lawrence Institute of Technology, School of Architecture
2100 West Ten Mile Road, Southfield, Michigan 48075
Karl H. Greimel, AIA, Dean   313 356-0200, ext. 172

Louisiana State University, School of Architecture
Baton Rouge, Louisiana 70803
A. Peters Oppermann, AIA, Director   504 388-6885

Louisiana Tech University, Department of Architecture
P.O. Box 3175 T.S., Ruston, Louisiana 71272
Peter Schneider, Head   318 257-2816

Maryland, University of, School of Architecture
College Park, Maryland 20742
John Ames Steffian, AIA, Dean   301 454-3427

Massachusetts Institute of Technology, Department of
Architecture, Cambridge, Massachusetts 02139
John R. Myer, FAIA, Head   617 253-7791

Miami, University of, School of Architecture
Coral Gables, Florida 33124
Nicholas N. Patricios, Interim Dean   305 284-3438

Miami University, Department of Architecture
Oxford, Ohio 45056
Ann Cline, Acting Chair   513 529-6426

Michigan, University of, College of Architecture and
Urban Planning, Ann Arbor, Michigan 48109
Robert C. Metcalf, FAIA, Dean   313 764-1300

Minnesota, University of, School of Architecture
Minneapolis, Minnesota 55455
Ralph Rapson, FAIA, Head   612 373-2198

Mississippi State University, School of Architecture
Mississippi State, Mississippi 39762
William G. McMinn, FAIA, Dean   601 325-2202

Montana State University, School of Architecture
Bozeman, Montana 59717
Robert C. Utzinger, AIA, Director   406 994-4255

Nebraska, University of, College of Architecture
Lincoln, Nebraska 68588
W. Cecil Steward, FAIA, Dean   402 472-3592

New Jersey Institute of Technology, School of
Architecture, Newark, New Jersey 07102
Sanford R. Greenfield, FAIA, Dean   201 645-5541

New Mexico, University of, School of Architecture and
Planning, Albuquerque, New Mexico 87131
George Anselevicius, AIA, Dean   505 277-2903

New York at Buffalo, State University of, School of
Architecture and Environmental Design
Buffalo, New York 14214
Robert G. Shibley, Chairman   716 831-3483

New York Institute of Technology, Center for Architecture
Old Westbury, New York 11568
Julio M. San Jose, Director   516 686-7593

North Carolina at Charlotte, University of
College of Architecture, Charlotte, North Carolina 28223
Charles C. Hight, AIA, Dean   704 597-2357

North Carolina State University, School of Design
P.O. Box 7701, Raleigh, North Carolina 27695-7701
Claude E. McKinney, Dean   919 737-2201

North Dakota State University, Department
of Architecture, Fargo, North Dakota 58105
Cecil D. Elliott, AIA, Chairman   701 237-8614

Notre Dame, University of, School of Architecture
Notre Dame, Indiana 46556
Robert L. Amico, AIA, Chairman   219 239-6137

Ohio State University, Department of Architecture
Columbus, Ohio 43210
Robert S. Livesey, Chairman   614 422-5567

Oklahoma, University of, College of Environmental Design
Norman, Oklahoma 73019
W. H. Raymond Yeh, AIA, Dean   405 325-2444

Oklahoma State University, School of Architecture
Stillwater, Oklahoma 74078
John H. Bryant, AIA, Head   405 624-6043

Oregon, University of, Department of Architecture
Eugene, Oregon 97403
Jerry V. Finrow, AIA, Head   503 686-3656

Pennsylvania, University of, Department of Architecture
Philadelphia, Pennsylvania 19104
Adele Naude Santos, Chairman   215 898-5728

Pennsylvania State University, Department of
Architecture, University Park, Pennsylvania 16802
Raniero Corbelletti, AIA, Head   814 865-9535

Pratt Institute, School of Architecture
200 Willoughby Avenue, Brooklyn, New York 11205
Paul Heyer, AIA, RIBA, Dean   212 636-3404

Princeton University, School of Architecture
Princeton, New Jersey 08540
Robert M. Maxwell, Dean   609 452-3737

Puerto Rico, University of, School of Architecture
San Juan, Puerto Rico 00931
Efrer Morales-Serrano, AIA, Dean   809 764-6040

Rensselaer Polytechnic Institute, School of Architecture
Troy, New York 12181
David S. Haviland, Dean   518 266-6460

Rhode Island School of Design, Division of Architectural
Studies, Providence, Rhode Island 02903
James Barnes, AIA, Acting Dean   401 331-3511

Rice University, School of Architecture
Houston, Texas 77001
O. Jack Mitchell, FAIA, Dean   713 527-4870

Southern California, University of, School of
Architecture, Los Angeles, California 90089
Robert S. Harris, AIA, Dean   213 743-2773

Southern California Institute of Architecture
1800 Berkeley Street, Santa Monica, California 90404
Raymond Kappe, FAIA, Director   213 829-3482

Southern University and A & M College, Division of
Architecture, Baton Rouge, Louisiana 70813
Arthur L. Symes, Director   504 771-3015

Southwestern Louisiana, University of, School of Art
and Architecture, Lafayette, Louisiana 70504
Dan P. Branch, AIA, Chairman   318 231-6624/6228

Syracuse University, School of Architecture
Syracuse, New York 13210
Werner Seligmann, Dean   315 423-2256

Temple University, Department of Architecture
Philadelphia, Pennsylvania 19122
George L. Claflen, Jr., AIA, Chairman   215 787-8826

Tennessee, University of, School of Architecture
Knoxville, Tennessee 37996-2400
Roy F. Knight, AIA, Dean   615 974-5265

Texas A & M University, Department of Architecture
College Station, Texas 77843
David Woodcock, Head   409 845-1015

Texas at Arlington, University of, School of
Architecture and Environmental Design
Box 19108, Arlington, Texas 76019
George S. Wright, AIA, Dean   817 273-2801

Texas at Austin, University of, School of Architecture
Austin, Texas 78712
Hal Box, FAIA, Dean   512 471-1922

Texas Tech University, Division of Architecture
Lubbock, Texas 79409
W. Lawrence Garvin, AIA, Chairman   806 742-3136

Tulane University, School of Architecture
New Orleans, Louisiana 70118
Ronald C. Filson, AIA, Dean   504 865-5389

Tuskegee Institute, Department of Architecture
Tuskegee Institute, Alabama 36088
Charles W. Raine, AIA, Assoc. Dean/Chairman   205 727-8329

Utah, University of, Graduate School of Architecture
Salt Lake City, Utah 84112
Robert L. Bliss, FAIA, Dean   801 581-8254

Virginia Polytechnic Institute and State University
College of Architecture and Urban Studies
Blacksburg, Virginia 24061
Charles W. Steger, Ph.D., AIA, Dean   703 961-6415

Virginia, University of, School of Architecture
Charlottesville, Virginia 22903
Jaquelin Taylor Robertson, FAIA, Dean   804 924-7019

Washington, University of, Department of Architecture
Seattle, Washington 98105
Robert Small, AIA, Chairman   206 543-4180

Washington State University, Department of Architecture
Pullman, Washington 99164
Robert J. Patton, AIA, Chairman   509 335-5539

Washington University, School of Architecture
Saint Louis, Missouri 63130
Constantine E. Michaelides, AIA, Dean   314 889-6200

Wisconsin-Milwaukee, University of, School of
Architecture and Urban Planning
Milwaukee, Wisconsin 53201
David Evan Glasser, AIA, Chairman   414 963-5337

Yale University, School of Architecture
New Haven, Connecticut 06520
Cesar Pelli, FAIA, Dean   203 436-0550